Born with a Spirit of Protest

Born with a Spirit of Protest

Giving Children a Voice of Importance

Craig Carpenter

Bullying – School Shootings – Eating
Disorders – Suicide

ROWMAN & LITTLEFIELD
Lanham • Boulder • New York • London

Published by Rowman & Littlefield
An imprint of The Rowman & Littlefield Publishing Group, Inc.
4501 Forbes Boulevard, Suite 200, Lanham, Maryland 20706
www.rowman.com

6 Tinworth Street, London SE11 5AL

British Library Cataloguing in Publication Information Available

Library of Congress Cataloging-in-Publication Data

ISBN 978-1-4758-5278-3 (cloth : alk. paper)
ISBN 978-1-4758-5279-0 (pbk.: alk. paper)
ISBN 978-1-4758-5280-6 (electronic)

∞ ™ The paper used in this publication meets the minimum requirements of American
National Standard for Information Sciences Permanence of Paper for Printed Library
Materials, ANSI/NISO Z39.48-1992.

To my parents: Leonard and Claribel Carpenter.
The most encouraging people I ever knew.

To the Mary Lou Fulton Department of Education at Arizona State
University: John Knaupp, PhD, Tom Barone, PhD, David Berliner, PhD,
who gave me the motivation to publish.

To the Doctorate of Ministry Staff at Drew University, who taught me
to think and write in narrative.

To my wife Marilyn, my support for over 50 years.

Table of Contents

Foreword

A sign of a civilized society is reflected in how its children are cared for. Are children offered opportunities for growth, safe places to play, learn and discover? Do countries and communities offer universal preschool, free childcare, quality healthcare, affordable housing, clean air and water, food that is free of pesticides and contaminants, and places to recreate?

Children assume they will be physically safe in schools, parks, churches, temples, synagogues, concert venues, malls, and airports. They assume that the adults in their lives will care for them, provide a safe space for them to grow, explore, question, and buffer them from adult problems that cause tensions across all social classes and communities.

Yet increasingly, youth across the country and globe are at risk of not experiencing a happy and safe childhood. We are bombarded on a daily basis with natural disasters, conflicts and civil war, economic downturns, erosion of the family, and the largest mass migration of capital, goods, and people since the end of the second world war.

Children are expected to grow up quickly, be aware, be vigilant, and not talk to strangers or linger.

They are increasingly socialized to be suspicious, instead of compassionate, and even preschoolers are conditioned, through active shooter drills, to be silent in order to be safe in school. These external mandates hijack childhood innocence and joy, especially in the United States. Counselors and school personnel share that children, exposed to images on social media, breaking news alerts, environmental destruction of homes and routines, serious adult issues, and witnesses to trauma, feel anxious. Teachers and schools tasked with reporting and supporting students encumbered by events that are not childhood concerns, note that there's not sufficient funds allocated to deal with the growing numbers of young people who require professional mental health services.

Children seem left to solitary solutions. Most young people think that no one else's story resonates with theirs.

But in the pages of this perceptive book, Craig Carpenter gently reminds them and us that other adolescents searched for answers as they, too, faced challenges and troubling events. The adults in their lives were unable to provide that safety net, quick-fix, or all-encompassing blanket of security to protect childhood and keep at bay the harshness that is often the world's experience.

Dr. Craig Carpenter provides readers with this heartfelt awareness: children may have lost their innocence, but not their sense of wonder. Through selected narratives of child authors, he gently reminds us that innovation, innate curiosity, and sense of discovery remain, in spite of tragedies, loss and difficult circumstances.

The initial chapters present a framework for the historical policies and regulations that affected children growing up during the American Revolution, the Civil War, westward expansion, industrialization, the civil rights movement, world wars and migrations.

Through narratives that are attentively crafted and written by young people, readers consider how a fair, just, and civilized society could not protect its youth—yet kids managed to survive and grow anyway.

The authentic narratives do not mince words. They situate us in the very places where the young authors experienced distress, betrayal, alienation, and destruction. The sobering stories in this collective work, capture our attention, activate our minds, and touch our hearts because of the young protagonists' determination, adaptability, and self-reliance.

Readers consider for a moment, that we are not alone in dealing with the daily psychological turbulence that occurs in our world, and, commonalities connect people, places, and environments across time, place, culture, and circumstance. The voices of the young authors cry out to us as their experiences illustrate universal themes of survival, loss, coming of age, finding your voice, and setting off on a new journey.

As a social studies educator and professor for nearly four decades, I noticed how teacher candidates and their students (K–12) are captivated by stories. Memorizing dates and random names are bland, distant and meaningless teaching strategies. However, when readers consider what it means to walk in the shoes of another and reflect upon the voices of young authors, whose stories are presented through richly descriptive prose, the place within themselves that researchers term "the text- to-self connection" is activated.

Dr. Carpenter knows that it's really all about writing and researching a book that kids relate to. How did someone their age cope, subvert, escape, and triumph?

What I most admire about this work is how it presents an historical timeline of what I term, "potholder topics"—historical events that are too hot to handle. Dr. Terrie Epstein (2009) notes that "a pedagogy of silence," persists when teachers and adults purposefully ignore, discourage, or avoid students' questions that deal with "uncomfortable" issues, events or concerns.

We all know that history repeats itself. So how do we assist young learners in making sense of people, programs and policies that cause harm? There is little comfort in offering "thoughts and prayers" or a moment of silence in the aftermath of tragedy, trauma or troubles. Anyone who has ever met a young child knows that they always ask, "Why?" Their search for answers propels them to discover for themselves.

Dr. Carpenter recognizes this essential element of child development and dedicated himself to researching voices of young people across time and place and writing an inspiring book that transcends disciplines.

Trauma is not limited to the classroom. Teacher candidates, doctoral students, professionals and practitioners across the health spectrum, from emergency medical technicians, to firefighters, counselors, social workers, psychologists, and special education directors witness the effects of childhood PTSD and neglect. While social media offers opportunities for children to be in touch with kids across town and across the globe, a pervasive emptiness persists, not only rooted in poverty, instability, or transiency, but through a sustained lack of acceptance—or the profound void of not belonging.

A colleague at my university supports victims and families of violent crime, through a federal grant. His task: reach out to children who have suffered trauma, exposure to violence, loss of a parent, loved one, or classmate, their own terminal illness, deportation, transiency, homelessness or depression.

Teachers and helping professionals can rely on this book to initiate discussion and stimulate kid-thinking. The child authors who share narratives of resolve, resiliency, and reinvention, in spite of policies, laws, entanglements, and circumstances beyond their control, assert hope for a better tomorrow. Readers who position themselves within the text can relate to the poignant narratives that authentically teach about how an issue, situation, policy, dictum, or decision affected a child in real time.

Dr. Carpenter reminds us why we study the past. The past sheds light on the present—and supports us in coping with injustice and unfair outcomes. This book reminds us that historically, kids have managed on their own, raised themselves and others, and dealt with traumatizing experiences. I don't think there's anyone who will be left untouched when reading the solitary accounts of children: growing, grieving, and seeking amazing grace

Born with a Spirit of Protest, is well-researched, relevant, and relatable. The activism and triumph of the youthful human spirit across centuries is a torch handed down to children and teens taking action now to change our world.

Barbara Torre Veltri, Ed. D.
Scottsdale, Arizona

REFERENCES

Epstein, T. (2009) Interpreting National History, Race, Identity, and Pedagogy in Classrooms and Communities. New York: Routledge.

Foreword

When children leave for school each morning unspoken expectations exist. Spontaneous, well-rehearsed movements of learning will take place in unabated routines. Parents and relatives drop their children off at school with the expectation that they will return. Parents depend on a myriad of committed, well-trained school personnel to teach and protect their children at school and safely return them at the end of the school day. Sadly, when a school shooting has taken place, not all children will return home.

In 2018, just one school year, nine school shootings took place. Fatalities were a tragic reality in each of them. FEMA reported ninety-four people who had been killed or injured. Life was lost, a new emphasis on school safety became a necessity, and a nation continues to grieve.

Communicating the "why" of a school shooting is a challenging task. The act is somewhat new to our historical past. The first shooting, creating national shock and attention, was Columbine in 1999. The word "shooting" was replaced with the word "massacre." The school library was the epicenter of thirteen murders and two suicides.

The premeditation, planning, and implementation of the calculated event was inconceivable. Included in the attack were three homemade bombs (two explosives that did not activate), twenty-five pipe bombs, ten propane bottles, two 9mm firearms, two twelve-gauge shotguns, a high-point 995 carbine, and a sawed off shotgun. The short-barreled firearms were equipped with high capacity magazines containing as many 52 rounds.

The goal was to inflict harm on as many students as possible in the shortest period of time. Since 2009 a total of 288 armed altercations have taken place. School shootings are becoming more frequent and are serious!

Professional strategies have flooded the airwaves, each one desperately attempting to provide a significant answer. Theories of prevention that involve outside reconstruction of doorways, identification cards that students are required to wear at all times, on-campus police presence, and safe stations for students and teachers during an actual shooting, as well as other helpful plans have been enacted. The Columbine tragedy also sparked serious debate. Topics of discussion about zero tolerance policies, gun control, the intimidation tactics of high school cliques, the subculture of social outcasts, both groups, gun culture, misuse of anti-depressants, internet use, and video game violence were at the forefront.

Encouragement groups, presented by Dr. Carpenter in this book, will work from the inside out increasing the number of eyes and ears available for detection. Encouragement groups within a school will also help with potential issues of eating disorders and thoughts of suicide.

Dr. Carpenter is an enthusiastic advocate of actuating the abilities of children. In the tradition of Alfred Adler, Rudolph Dreikurs, John Dewey and Maria Montessori, Carpenter believes that children are significantly more capable than what adults believe them to be, subscribing to the notion that children will show responsibility when they are given important tasks of responsibility. Involvement in an encouragement group gives students the opportunity to make a significant contribution to the well-being of others.

Responsibility entrusted to children can be seen in the participation of children in historical contexts. Major events such as the Revolutionary War, the women's movement, the civil rights movement, the Vietnam War, Occupy Wall Street, gay rights, and the "March For Our Lives" are examples cited by Dr. Carpenter. Children played a vital role in the success of these historical precedents as well as many others.

Dr. Carpenter reminds us that the Postmodern Movement, a change in the direction of the perspectives in society, confronted the perfectionist constructs of Modernism. Carpenter explains how the greed of the Enlightenment entrepreneurs, the inhumane treatment of workers during the Industrial Revolution, and the psychological/physical carnage of two world wars impacted the issues of working toward world cooperation. The movement also was a pretext for the acknowledgment and use of the skills of children to accomplish important tasks.

This book comprehensibly discusses the important contribution of the Romantics who brought the human element to the forefront. One of the most important themes has to do with the way reality is perceived. New understandings of dignity, within the life struggles of ordinary people, are discussed in life scenarios.

Dr. Carpenter states, "What used to be considered universal truth is now divided into many truths. Postmodernism protests any scientific language, religious belief, political claim or any anything else that defines itself as ultimate. From the perspective of post-moderns, universal Truth (capital T) is not germane. Rather, many truths (small t) that are specific to a society or group of people are relevant. That is to say, postmodernism vehemently rejects grand narratives that claim to have 'Ultimate Truth.'"

The manuscript entices the reader to take a journey into the creative thoughts, ideas, and strategies of children to solve problems. The content gradually transports the reader into stories about vivid accounts of life challenges, clothed in courage and creativity. Postmodern children see themselves as equals in their own challenges for over-coming life obstacles.

Dr. Carpenter uses the medium of narratives (stories) to communicate the similarities between all children in their quest to overcome challenges. He states, "The children of today are fully aware that everyone has something to contribute: parents, teachers, relatives, friends and people from different countries of origin. They have a renewed energy to learn through the stories (narratives) of others and to share their own encounters with the unpredictable events of life. Postmodern children view themselves as individuals, peers and members of a local and world community."

Throughout the book, the reader is confronted with factual accounts about children. The accounts, grip the reader with emotion and disbelief. The reader becomes an active spectator as life events transform into emotional and sometimes physical pain. The book underscores the traumatic situations that students face as they discover the emotional pain associated with attempting to find a place of belonging among peers. When students participate in an encouragement group immediate acceptance and recognition takes place.

Dr. Carpenter emphasizes the strategic role of encouragement in a child's life. He points out that adults, without fully realizing it, actually contribute to the discouragement of children. Discouragement begins when adults fail to realize that children have the natural and acquired skills to participate co-equally with adults to make mutual decisions. Since misbehavior occurs in the social settings of life, children can solve common problems in the social interactions they experience at school. With guidance, students can contribute to one another providing support and strategies to deal with negative encounters.

Discouragement is identified as the precursor to negative interactions with other people inhabiting the world of students. When discouragement is dominate in a student's life two responses will likely occur; the child will lash out in the direction of others or withdraw showing actions of self-harm. According to Dr. Carpenter, encouragement groups become a source of shared strategies as students begin to understand that everyone has obstacles to overcome.

The reader is confronted, from the beginning of the book to its conclusion, with a real-time experience of a school shooting and its aftermath. *Born with a Spirit of Protest,* concludes with a narrative that leaves the reader in the same quandary as a deeply discouraged student attempting to make a rational decision in a hurtful environment. When students are constantly barraged with negative comments from fellow peers, animosity in varying degrees is the natural result.

Encouragement groups give students a natural outlet to discuss everyday experiences, both positive and negative. The supportive nature of encouragement groups gives participants new and creative ideas for discussing and surviving hurtful circumstances rather than remaining angry.

Dr. Carpenter's timely book is a must read for anyone involved with children and adolescence, including parents and educators across many disciplines such as Education, Social Work, Criminal Justice, Psychology and many others. *Born with a Spirit of Protest* presents relevant information to anyone on the receiving end of bullying as well as the perpetrators who bully. It also leaves the reader with information about the devastation of discouragement and the behavior choices it influences.

Ellen E. Whipple, PhD, ACSW
Associate Professor
School of Social Work
Michigan State University

Preface

"A deed knocks first at thought." —Emily Dickinson

This book is primarily about children and democracy. It requires thinking outside the box (as the quote by Emily Dickinson insinuates) with regard to creating situations of usefulness for children. This book is not specifically about discipline in the classroom, community–school relationships, academic testing, or a critique of education; it is nonetheless about tapping into a resource that is often overlooked by parents, teachers, and community leaders.

The American pragmatist philosopher John Dewey (2005) believed that democratic values could be attained only through knowledge and experience. That is to say, children can hear about the democratic process by listening to a lecture, observe it by watching political news or a political debate, and learn about it by reading a book, but it was Dewey's belief that children cannot fully grasp the effectiveness of democracy and its powerful influence unless they experience it.

When children and adolescents are given the opportunity to participate in democratic discussions, they quickly learn that most problems are created and solved in the social settings of life. It was Dewey's belief that the solving process begins with experience. Dewey (2005) states, "When we experience something, we act upon it, we do something with it" (152).

We live in a nation of democratic principles. They are foremost in our minds. They stir the compassion in our hearts and they maintain our historical perspectives. More often than not, however, children and adolescents are left out of the democratic process until they are adults, when they can vote. When children are permitted to actively participate in discussion-oriented decision making, the motivation to learn is increased, skill sets for cooperative behavior are developed, and the fair treatment of others becomes an approach to life that effectively eliminates bullying and other needless power struggles.

In each election cycle, various states consider lowering the voting age to increase voter participation. Voting, however, is not an event; it is a lifestyle. Understanding the community logic of today's children and adolescents is crucial in activating the democratic process with them.

This book applauds democratic discussions as a profound influence on children. It presents the case that children and adolescents are fully capable to participate in discussion-based democracy at home, at school, and in other settings. Today's children are community driven, thriving on the idea of working together to solve problems.

For children and adolescents, the practices of democracy create an authentic forum for cooperation, community feeling, and informed participation. When children and adolescents are given a say, *it does not necessarily mean they get their way*—which is true in a democracy as well.

A child's natural desire is to experience a place of belonging. The child's goals in life are formed from it. The child's behavior choices in social settings are pointed out by it. And the child's contribution to others is motivated from it.

Young (1965) accurately depicts mistaken perceptions of parents about children. Young describes one particular misconception of adults about each new generation of children: that "the new batch of children is a cut below the standard of their own youthful days. Many were doubtful about the current offspring which, in turn, generated doubt about the future status of the world."

Young goes on to discuss the fact that some improvement has transpired and that the current generation—now adults—weren't really remiss in the goals they set and reached: "But it's likely that adults . . . have created their own fantasies about what children ought to be like…It is one of those sleight-of-hand tricks that can be very convenient and that ends up causing endless trouble and confusion" (2).

Today's children believe that differing points of view can be valid and are skeptical of bias, especially one bias in particular: that children and adolescents are not mature enough to initiate and follow through on discussion-based decisions. The children and adolescents of today see it quite differently, believing they will be able to accept important responsibilities when given the chance.

Historically, protest has been incited when people were not included in decisions that impacted their lives. More often than not, these decisions were made using dictatorial tactics and the people who were affected decided to fight back. Sometimes it was an armed rebellion, as witnessed in the Revolutionary War. Many times, it was nonviolent protests like those seen in the civil rights movement, demonstrations opposing the war in Vietnam, the Occupy Wall Street movement, and the march on Washington, DC, initiated by the students from Marjory Stoneman Douglas High School.

College-age students have numerous avenues of objection. Children, however, have very few venues to share ideas, strategies, or disagreements. Too often, they become discouraged, resorting to power-struggle tactics: drugs, poor academic performance, lack of cooperation, and bullying. Effective democratic living demands the recognition of equality, regardless of age.

The March for Our Lives on Washington, DC, in 2018 was a protest against gun violence, more specifically high-capacity assault rifles, and the National Rifle Association. It was a coequal involvement between children and adults. Adults, however, had very little participation in the actual march and the speeches that followed it. It was a prime example of democracy in action. The march revealed the ability of students to give a voice of importance.

Introduction

February 14, 2018, presented itself as a typical day in the desert of Arizona. Darkness surrendered to the spectacle of blue sky and sunshine without obvious struggle or hindrance. The hourly increase in warmth was timely and predictable. Birds were melodically chirping.

Leaves from summer and fall, serving as protective foliage, fluttered downward as gravity gently tugged at the remaining core of their seasonal existence. The distant drone of lawn equipment murmured a familiar lullaby of haste as loyal workers manicured green lawns, briskly shined southwestern yard art, and skillfully persuaded remnant particles of waste to join the others already gathered.

It was slated to be the international day of love, a celebration of mystery that only the heart could ever scribe into intimate words of meaning. Sales of scented flowers, sweetened candy, and romantic prose would light up the computers at checkout lines in local stores.

At a robotic pace, I touched the button that brought the K-Cup coffee maker to life, retrieved my fresh cup of coffee, ambled toward the couch, and maneuvered my free hand to remotely awaken the television from sleep to action mode. I drained the cup of coffee and reached for my laptop. It was a familiar drill that produced success each morning.

I was arduously toiling over the final chapter of this book. I worked nonstop for a few hours, barely hearing the continuous cycle of news, when the heart-sinking announcement came: "There is breaking news out of Florida. Another school shooting has taken place. One reported death and multiple injuries. We now take you to Parkland, Florida . . ."

Only one death, I thought. One too many, but it could have been worse. Little did I know that the innocence of childhood had been abruptly interrupted by the arrogance of death seventeen times, leaving behind the carnage of shock, hurt, and torrid memories that would reverberate through the survivors' lives.

My mind began to drift, traveling to a place it had journeyed too many times before. It was a place of imagined reality.

The high school students paraded from the school with hands held in awkward positions. Some of the kids were grasping for the shoulders of the person in front of them. Others held their hands up. Many appeared distraught and confused with surreal looks of numbed bewilderment. No doubt an authority figure was trying to tell them what to do. A number of them had likely started the day spending harried time in a tiled shower stall.

The well-rehearsed next stop would be to a vinyl stool, surrounded by mirrors and a tray of eyeliner, lip gloss, and mascara in organized disarray, or perhaps standing with a razor, lathered with scents designed for young men coming of age. Sadly, for some, it would be the last time they were awakened by an annoying alarm or the magnified voice of a parent.

Death had begun its relentless stalk. In a short period of time a cold, lifeless statistic would be reported.

My imaginative journey continued. Varied means of transportation delivered scores of students to the school. Friends greeted one another as they scurried to their first classes. Angst was a dominant emotion, as cards of romantic expression would be distributed at some point during the day. Cherished moments of acceptance, affirmation, and innocent embarrassment lay ahead. At least, that was the plan.

Unexpectedly, something went very wrong. Sounds of normalcy were transformed into panicked reverberations of chaos as gun shots replaced the noise of learning. The wrinkled countenance of parents—praying, crying, and waiting for a report that would either crush their spirits or allow them to hug their children another time—was alarming to view.

The death of any child is wounding to the very soul of our existence. The dreaded news eventually surfaced, as it always does. First responders performed their duties as their cerebral faces camouflaged broken hearts and disbelief. No doubt they forced themselves to perform their duties as best they could. Perhaps, the responders received training in disassociation mental techniques (disconnected from the here and now), but this event was the real thing.

Loved ones were finally notified, and they cried. Parents cried. Brothers and sisters cried. Grandparents cried. Cousins cried. Friends cried. And God wept.

Delayed discussions and romanticized future plans—family excursions, birthday parties, graduation ceremonies, wedding days, the birth of children, and myriad other events—were painfully lost in a split second of evil incarnate.

The grief process birthed agonizing "if only" scenarios, followed by over-whelming guilt: If only I had hugged her longer; if only I had replaced that lecture on responsibility with an extended high five; if only I had said "I'm proud of you" instead of "you need to," or "I love you" instead of "I'm annoyed at you"; if only we knew ahead of time and could have done something different; if only it were possible to freeze-frame a life. In later years, a look at family photos would include the tearful words, "But one picture is missing." The sands of life were shifting and out of control.

No words exist—no words will will ever exist—that can heal the emotional pain of the parents whose children were egregiously taken from them, forever. The death of a child is, and will always be, excruciating to the heart.

The perpetrator became the immediate subject of a thousand queries: How did he get a gun? Why was he allowed to buy a gun? Why were his statements not taken seriously? Obviously, his mental condition had slipped through the cracks as he slowly spiraled into a very dark and demented place.

Politicians filled the airways in repeated verbal volleys, siding with and against one another. Promises were once again constructed by professional wordsmiths, while the capable students of Marjory Stoneman Douglas High School were transforming loss into protests that would stir the hearts of a nation.

From the courageous view points of the students, they were taking action so life would never again surrender to death from gun violence. Brave parents and teachers, looking pale after uncountable hours of disbelief, took the microphones in support of all parents everywhere, uttering a commitment to camaraderie: "We have your back. We will never let this happen to you."

The theme of this book is that children are capable beyond what we believe them to be. Even before the 2018 March for Our Lives, children have been at the forefront of amazing creativity. The march in Washington, DC, was almost beyond comprehension: coming together at what seemed to be lightning speed, more organized than many political rallies, and performed before a world audience.

High school students communicated meaningful messages that were energizing to the mind, heart and soul: *Politicians believe that the right to own a gun comes before our lives. Get ready to be voted out by us. Enough is enough. We are the change.* One speaker was silent for six minutes, the amount of time it took to kill seventeen of their classmates and teachers. They were joined by other protesters in other cities and overseas. Children and adolescents are significantly more capable than we believe them to be!

Educators continue to face formidable challenges: solving social issues among children, developing motivational curriculum, and training in classroom management so they can create environments for optimal learning. Often, top-down strategies are the only ones used to improve conditions.

Experts and specialists are frequently contracted by school districts to give advice and are usually well-versed in their areas of specialty. A resource that is often overlooked is the contribution of children. The involvement of students, using discussion-oriented problem solving, is significantly under-utilized.

Children can be useful in many aspects of life at school. They observe and experience discussions from the time they can first communicate. Children observe opinionated discourses, animated disagreements, respectful negotiations, and practical problem solving. Discussion-based involvement becomes natural to them. Unfortunately, opportunities at school, in the community, and at home are often—mistakenly—delayed. Therefore, helpful information from children about numerous subjects remains unheard, and possible solutions remain elusive.

A crucial addition to solving the problem of gun violence is the formation of encouragement groups. Encouragement groups help students to stay engaged with one another. Elementary, middle school, and high school students are fully capable of including all peers in a small-group setting where the central goal is encouragement. Encouragement groups can completely stop school shootings.

The purpose of this book is to show that children and adolescents are fully capable of preventing gun violence in schools through encouragement groups. The chapters herein present the idea that students are in a position to wield formidable influence on preventing school violence.

Each chapter of the book builds on the previous chapter. The preface communicates the spirit of democracy inherent in adults and children. It is meant to motivate the quest for greater adult participation in the democratic process and to energize children in the same direction. Encouragement groups give children and adolescents a forum to practice democratic principles with one another as well as with teachers and administrators.

Chapter 1 discusses six historical events that resulted from protest movements, highlighting the important role of children. The historical events discussed are: the Revolutionary War, the women's movement, the civil rights movement, the Vietnam War, Occupy Wall Street, LGBTQ rights, and the March for Our Lives. Each of these events shows the skills and the courage of children in action.

Chapter 2 conveys the pertinent influences on the development of the postmodern movement. This chapter underscores the viewpoints of the philosopher-scientists and the contrary perspectives of the Romantics. The Enlightenment and the false promises of modernism are also examined. Included in this chapter is the role of classic literature and its contribution to the principles of the postmodern movement. Postmodernism rescued children from the notion that children "should be seen and not heard" as adults began to see that students possessed the skill sets to solve varied problems and contribute to the greater good in settings where students live and grow.

A brief exegesis is written about the role of the following novels in the development of postmodernism: *Oliver Twist* (loss of human dignity), *The Jungle* (unhealthy working conditions), *All Quiet on the Western Front* (isolation), *The Grapes of Wrath* (rugged individualism), *Night* (the Holocaust), *Rabbit, Run* (the replacement of traditional values), and *To Kill A Mockingbird* (prejudice). Each of these novels humanized obstacles in life, which in turn cultivated an atmosphere that enabled children to contribute to solving life challenges.

Chapter 3 emphasizes the postmodern notion of narrative (stories) as a way to communicate real accounts of survival in the greater community in which children live. Postmodern children see themselves as coequal in their own challenges. Some of the stories are historical in content, while others are stories about the capabilities of children as they courageously contribute to others.

Chapter 4 shows the abilities of children in problem-solving situations. Examples of skillful participation are given, offering insight into the effective use of small groups, democratic principles, and encouragement in the classroom. Also included are current metaphors that schools are striving to activate: school as community, school as belonging, school as encouragement, school as spirituality, school as participation.

Chapter 5 provides information regarding possible causes and solutions to the problem of bullying. Topics discussed are family modeling, feelings of inferiority, approach to life, birth order dynamics, social interest, and creating communities of imperfection. As previously mentioned, a strategic addition to the solving gun violence is the formation of encouragement groups.

Encouragement groups help students keep track of one another. Elementary, middle school, and high school students are fully capable of recruiting and leading students to a small group where the central goal is the emotional health of each participant. That students were able to form an international protest march is proof of the ability of students to form small groups. *Children are capable!*

Chapter One

The Role of Children in Historical Events

"Man is born free, yet he is everywhere in chains."—Jean-Jacques Rousseau

Children born in the United States immediately after the Revolutionary War, as well as the generations to come, were born with a spirit of protest. It appears in the child's perspective shortly after birth. The legacy of personal opinions, regardless of age, runs deep in the child's rational and emotional veins.

Children, similar to their opinionated parents, desire to participate in contributing to the greater good as well as solving everyday problems. Historian David McCullough (2001) writes about a Revolutionary War–era confrontation "on an icy, cobbled square where the Province House stood, a lone British sentry, posted in front of the nearby custom house was being taunted by a small band of men and boys" (p. 65).

HISTORICAL ROOTS

A brief history of notable protest movements and the role of children in them follows. At the very least, in these movements children were firsthand observers; in many instances they were given vital jobs.

The Revolutionary War

Undoubtedly, the most historic protest movement in the United States resulted in the Revolutionary War. Prior to the war, many settlers came to North America to escape religious persecution from theocratic rulers in Europe. Others were simply hungry for new adventures in a new land, and a sizable group of people were frustrated with political inequality. Once the new inhabitants were effectively organized, regardless of their original motive, protests against absolute rule emerged. The Revolutionary War was the eventual outcome.

The war became a mutual effort. The men became soldiers while the women ran the farms. Some women sewed the uniforms, others followed the troops as cooks and chefs, those with medical skills served as nurses to the wounded, and a considerable group made gunpowder and cannon balls. Children were also involved. Hakim (1993) writes, "Children were part of it, too. An observer in Massachusetts watched children making cartridges, running bullets, making soldiers' wallets (soldiers' bags) and baking biscuit (soldiers' food)" (p. 108).

Children were given useful assignments of significance. Some children carried rifles, but most were shielded from battle. They were, however, immersed in the spirit of protest that existed in the fight for independence. Making cartridges and soldiers' bags and distributing food were strategic to winning the war. Reliance on children was a key factor.

The Women's Movement

Many of the earliest events of the women's movement transpired during the slavery years of American history, especially in the South. Men played the dominant role in society in academics, finance, medicine, and vocational tasks. Ministers used the Bible not only to justify slavery but also to keep women in their proper place. The virtuous Christian woman of the South remained at home, showing submission, spirituality, and affection.

In the North, many women would have nothing to do with this. The practice was so abhorrent to them that their crusade, which started out to abolish slavery, also became a crusade to end forced sex among slave women; mixed-race children were plentiful. Groups of women were quickly formed and gained formidable influence. Susan B. Anthony (1859) wrote with fervor, "Mothers, I appeal to you. Half the slaves are women, helpless, defenseless creatures, with no law, no religion, no public sentiment to shield them from the sensual Simon Legrees who hunt them" (p. 161).

Groups of women flooded congress with petitions demanding the termination of slavery in the nation's capital. Women also demanded the end of the discriminatory practice of forbidding interracial marriages. Lydia Maria Child (1839) explained, "The legalized contempt of color in Massachusetts . . . [directly] sustains slavery in the South, and is publicly quoted for that purpose" (p. 161).

And finally, women's groups toiled to create a speaking circuit for women. In May 1838, Angelina Grimké, Lucretia Mott, and Abby Kelley Foster spoke before three thousand people in Philadelphia. A hostile mob outside the hall began to smash the windows outside as Grimké stood to speak. According to William Lloyd Garrison (1838), the mob only improved her charismatic speaking style: "Her eyes flashed, and her cheeks glowed" (p. 162). Since women, for the most part, were still responsible for the children, the women's audiences were often mixed groups of women and children.

The children of these reformers observed what was happening in a society that favored men. They understood the lack of equality for women.

Children were within hearing distance of volatile discussions, sight distance of both angry and supportive audiences, and walking distance to the gathered audiences. Experiencing the epicenter of the protest movement brought to light the struggles involved with combating grand narratives that were used to keep marginalized people trapped. According to Walters (1976) the importance of children was becoming germane: "The child was coming into its own in literature; . . . debate over the correct kind of education to give children in schools and at home in order to guarantee they would become a force for good."

Two noteworthy publications were created for children. The South produced *The Slave's Friend,* which warned its youthful readers "not to throw it down . . ." and candidly informed them that it was not written "merely to amuse them" (Walters, 1976, p. 96–97). "*The Child's Newspaper,*" a communication of the North, promised to tell "of things that are taking place in the world" (p. 96–97).

The mission would continue, with victories and defeats, but the courage of women refused to subside. In 1848, Seneca Falls, New York, hosted the first women's rights convention. The outcome was a Declaration of Sentiments signed by sixty-eight women and thirty-two men, as well as twelve resolutions calling for equal treatment of women and men under the law, including voting rights for women. Quarles (1969) quotes a summation by Abby Kelley Foster: "We have good cause to be grateful to the slave, in striving to strike *his* chains off, we found, most surely, that *we* were manacled ourselves" (p. 248).

In May 1869 Anthony and Elizabeth Cady Stanton formed the National Woman Suffrage Association with the goal of achieving voting rights for women through a constitutional amendment. More than fifty years later, on August 26, 1920, Secretary of State Bainbridge Colby signed into law the Nineteenth Amendment, giving women the right to vote.

The children of these reformers would carry the women's movement into the decades to follow. The new obstructions they would face were every bit as formidable: birth control, personal decisions about abortion, equal pay, educational opportunities, and a phenomenon known as the glass ceiling. A spirit of protest would continue when these children became adults, regardless of the obstacles. Today's children are cultural and generational recipients of an era where protest movements were observable events. The events were documented in pictures by photographers, written in textbooks and discussed in textbooks.

The Civil Rights Movement

In 1955 Rosa Parks, a black person, refused to give up her seat to a white person on a city bus in Montgomery, Alabama. Parks simply wanted to be treated as coequal in a democratic society. Her courageous act began a tidal wave of boycotts and demonstrations against the bus system. After a fairly short—but difficult—period of time using other means of transportation (mostly walking), black people were allowed to sit wherever they chose.

In 1963 Dr. Martin Luther King Jr. began the most discernible parts of the civil rights movement. Other civil rights activists were working behind the scenes. Black people in the South joined King in an unprecedented attempt to be treated as coequal under the Constitution, with the same rights that were given to white citizens. Thousands of people watched the protests on television. King's influence, as well that of others, changed an entire system of government that lacked equality for all of its citizens.

During the turbulent year of 1963, both adults and children participated in the marches. The Selma to Montgomery march and the March on Washington were notable protests. As a result, black Americans were, for the most part allowed to vote, join together in public places, avoid discrimination in trade unions and schools, find jobs prohibiting sexual discrimination, attend integrated schools, and benefit from the Equal Employment Opportunity Commission.

Turck (2000) describes the struggle of an all-black high school in 1947. Located in Farmville, a town in Prince Edward County, Virginia, the school was overcrowded. Three tar paper shacks—essentially nothing more than wooden structures with black paper draped over them—were built by the county to serve as temporary classrooms. The school was devoid of a cafeteria, student lockers, central heating, a microscope, and reliable school buses.

Barbara Johns was a student council member who was fed up with the school conditions she and her fellow students were forced to endure. She stated her frustrations with her friends, and the students began meeting in secret. The move they were about to make was risky and dangerous, but they knew they were entitled to improved school conditions and an equal education. "They also knew the dangers of commanding anything from the white people who ran the county government. They thought about the danger they would face if they acted and the injustice that they suffered, so long as no one acted. Then all 450 students followed Johns out of school and on strike" (Turck, 1999, p. 10).

Johns was taking a huge risk, both emotionally and physically. When anyone—children or adults—protested the established order, they were at the mercy of authority figures. It is likely that Johns had witnessed or heard stories of black Americans who experienced beatings, verbal threats, or even death as they crusaded for the cause of equality. Perhaps well-meaning relatives, neighbors, and friends attempted to persuade her to cancel her protest. No lawyers or organizations were available to her if she was arrested. The only thing she had to rely on was her courage. Barbara Johns was only sixteen years old. And the protest worked—soon after the walk-out the school board began working on school improvements and eventually plans for a newer building.

The Vietnam War

In the late 1960s and early 1970s, the Vietnam War spawned a protest movement after federal government instituted a draft, forcing individuals to join the fighting forces. Numerous protests emerged, with war-eligible individuals marching as a sign of resistance. Draft cards were burned, sit-ins were commonplace, university administration offices were occupied, and, sadly, on May 4, 1970, four students were shot and killed at Kent State University. The protests had a significant influence on the end of the war.

The protesters were almost entirely composed of college, university, and high school students. French photojournalist Marc Riboud describes a young woman who was seventeen: "She was just talking; trying to catch the eye of the soldiers, maybe trying to have a dialogue with them. . . . I had the feeling the soldiers were more afraid of her than she was of the bayonets" (Curry, 2004).

"I was a good heart trying to follow the light," the girl recalled. "I just hopped on a D.C. transit bus and went down to join the revolution. None of this was planned" (Curry 2004).

The Vietnam War was unpopular. Television cameras exposed lurid scenes of death, destruction, and carnage. Body bags, along with the names of dead soldiers, were a common feature in newscasts. It was also considered a rich man's war, since those eligible to be drafted were given a deferment for attending college.

Protesters were often shown as victims of water assaults, aggressive police dogs, rubber bullets, toxic spray, and, in the protest at Kent State University, even death from live rounds of ammunition. It was dangerous to be a protester, yet thousands of students participated in rallies and marches.

Occupy Wall Street

A more recent protest movement became known as Occupy Wall Street, later branching into the larger Occupy movement. Although the protest seemed to lack the organization of other movements, it was still newsworthy. The objective was to bring attention to corporate greed and dishonesty, often sustained by the political process.

Hundreds of people, mostly college students and young college graduates, in 12 cities camped out in financial districts expressing disenchantment and frustration with unemployment, monumental student debt, and unfair tax benefits to the corporate sector. Essentially, participants pointed out that democracy could not thrive in a society operated solely for the benefit of the rich and powerful. Sandel (2012) writes, "In the fall of 2011, the Occupy Wall Street Movement brought protests to cities throughout the United States and around the world. These protests targeted big banks and corporate power, and the rising inequality of income and wealth" (p. 12).

LGBTQ Rights

Similar to women's quest for equal rights, the LGBTQ rights movement had analogous incentives and faced similar opposition. When protests against women increased, so did their resolve for fair treatment. Movements against LGBTQ people had the same result, serving to intensify their desire for equality. Marone (2003) writes, "The gay rights movement began—we can affix an exact date of June 27, 1969" (p. 444). A police raid on the Stonewall Inn, a popular gay bar in Greenwich Village, escalated into a riot that served as the catalyst for gay and lesbian people to unite under the banner of the Gay Liberation Front.

A profound movement led by adolescents is the gay-straight alliance, which has been promoted as an intervention strategy to make school environments safer and more inclusive by a number of national organizations, including the American Civil Liberties Union (ACLU), GLSEN (formerly the Gay, Lesbian, and Straight Education Network), the Human Rights Campaign (HRC), Human Rights Watch, the National LGBTQ Task Force, and many others.

In February 2007, small group of adults attended a San Diego School District meeting to complain about the participation of San Diego charter schools in the city's Gay Pride parade. Critics claimed it exposed children to pornographic scenes, sexual imagery, and overt displays of affection between homosexuals. San Diego school superintendent Carl H. Cohn presided over the meeting and declared that he had no objections to the students' participation. Not one parent at the meeting or in the school district objected to it. either.

On June 26, 2015, a US Supreme Court ruling established same-sex marriage across the United States. Justice Anthony Kennedy (2015) wrote,

> No union is more profound than marriage, for it embodies the highest ideals of love, fidelity, devotion, sacrifice and family. In forming a marital union, two

people become something greater than once they were. As some of the peti-tioners in these cases demonstrate, marriage embodies a love that may endure even past death. It would misunderstand these men and women to say they disrespect the idea of marriage. Their plea is that they do respect it, respect it so deeply that they seek to find its fulfillment for themselves. Their hope is not to be condemned to live in loneliness, excluded from one of civilizations oldest institutions. They asked for equal dignity in the eyes of the law. The Constitution grants them that right. The judgment of the court of appeals for the Sixth Circuit is reversed. *It is so ordered.* (p. 49)

Gay people were (and in some places still are) considered the scourge of humanity. They were victims of egregious name-calling and were mistakenly blamed for the entirety of the AIDS epidemic. Even to this day, many people, especially in the Bible Belt states, continue to struggle with LGBTQ issues.

Many church denominations condemned homosexuality with the same animosity as blatantly violating the Ten Commandments. Denominational factions developed over the correct interpretation of scripture. Some gay people, as depicted in the 2005 film *Brokeback Mountain*, were beaten and killed simply because of their sexual orientation.

It took unbelievable courage to come out as a gay person during this era of heightened condemnation of homosexuality. Friends and relatives—espe-cially grandparents—were instrumental in turning the tide of negative per-ceptions with organizations like PFLAG (formerly Parents, Families and Friends of Lesbians and Gays). LGBTQ students and allies banded together in gay-straight alliance groups at school and marched in Gay Pride parades.

The March for Our Lives

On February 14, 2018, another school shooting took place. A former student from Marjory Stoneman Douglas High School, armed with an AR-15 semi-automatic rifle, opened fire on unsuspecting students in the hallway at the school. Seventeen people were killed.

With flowing tears and broken hearts, the students bravely decided to fight back. Using nonviolent protest, high school students marched on the Florida state legislature as well as the United States Capitol in support of stricter gun control. In Washington, D.C., approximately eight hundred thou-sand people were in attendance, mostly high school students. Students in hundreds of communities around the world, who did not go to Washington D.C., walked out of classrooms and organized demonstrations within their own communities.

All of the speakers were teenagers. Adults were not allowed to speak from the podium. David Hogg, a Parkland shooting survivor, said, "We are going to make this the voting issue. We are going to take this to every election, to every state and every city" (Segarra, 2018)

Protest movements in the twentieth and twenty-first centuries have influenced laws and policies on issues as varied as Prohibition, Jim Crow laws, the rights of women and minorities to vote, purity codes, immigration, anti-evolution laws, the role of women in the workplace, and reproductive choice, and have highlighted the issues surrounding just and unjust wars, unequal wealth distribution and tax codes, and gun control. If it were possible to compact the aforementioned movements into a phrase, it would read: "the struggle for equality."

The desire for equality is woven into the fabric of our being. We understand what this means for adults, but what are the implications for children in the democratic process? Is it possible to include children in more situations at school, home, and the community than just homework assignments, household chores, and classroom rules? Today's children, like the children of the past, desire a voice of importance.

Voices of importance, similar to the voices of the aforementioned examples, are central to the success of encouragement groups. Elementary, middle school, and high school students will notice the positive changes in other students as they communicate words of encouragement to one another. Adults can work at noticing positive changes and comment on them.

Chapter Two

The Postmodern Movement

New Opportunities for Children

"I have decided to use the word *postmodern* to describe that condition. . . . [I]t designates the state of our culture following the transformations which, since the end of the nineteenth century, have altered the rules. . . . I define postmodernism as incredulity toward meta-narratives."—Jean-François Lyotard

Today's children live in a postmodern world. Postmodernism has been in process since the conclusion of World War II. It has been examined, scrutinized, and discussed in books, journals, and magazines to such an extent that some experts suggest the use of a new term, post-postmodernism. Many intellectuals have moved past it.

ELEMENTS OF POSTMODERNISM

Postmodernism is a belief that all people share both commonality and uniqueness. The commonality is that of participation, belonging, and contribution to a local and larger community. This is accomplished by respecting the uniqueness of persons or groups according to religion, culture, and moral perspective. In order to do this, however, viewpoints needed to change from exclusion to inclusion in both national and local decisions. French philosopher Michel Foucault (1989) gives the following example, "I label political everything that has to do with class struggle and social everything that derives from and is a consequence of the class struggle, expressed in human relationships and in institutions" (p. 104). What used to be considered universal truth is now divided into many truths. Postmodernism protests any scientific language, religious belief, political claim, or anything else that defines itself as ultimate. From the perspective of postmoderns, there is no universal Truth (capital T) but rather many truths (lowercase t) that are specific to particular societies or groups of people. That is to say, postmodernism vehemently rejects grand narratives and claims to "ultimate Truth."

The postmodern movement gives children more opportunities to participate in discussion-based forums, since varied perspectives are equal in their possibilities. The children of today are fully aware that everyone has something to contribute: parents, teachers, relatives, friends, and people from different countries of origin.

Students are energized by the stories (narratives) of others and desire to share their own encounters with the unpredictable events of life. Postmodern children view themselves as individuals, peers, and members of a local and world community.

Origins of Postmodernism

In order to understand the origins of postmodernism, it is essential to understand the philosophical backstory that was influential in creating its narrative. A brief look at the historical events prior to the postmodern philosophical movement—namely, the Enlightenment and the Industrial Revolution in both Europe and the United States—will aid this understanding.

The narrative begins with the discoveries and corresponding promises of the philosopher-scientists. A brief glimpse into the philosophical-scientific thinking is helpful in grasping the reactionary nature of postmodernity.

Magee (1998) discusses the findings that were deemed as *ultimate* by the philosopher-scientists. Isaac Newton introduced science as mechanical properties applying laws to all objects moving on the surface of the earth. Francis Bacon (1561–1626) is considered the godfather of science. He was one of the first philosopher-scientists to suggest that scientific inquiry could actually give humankind ultimate power over nature.

According to Bacon, only science could drive prosperity to unimaginable heights. Thomas Hobbes (1588–1679) believed that physical matter was all that existed. Everything could be explained in the scientific construct of matter in motion. Hobbes viewed the mind as a machine, just as the universe is nothing more than a machine governed by matter. Hobbes agreed with Galileo that science was ultimate truth, replacing reasonless faith in God.

Postmodern philosopher Richard Rorty (1998) suggested that "we give up the correspondence theory of truth and start treating moral and scientific beliefs as tools for achieving greater human happiness, rather than as representations of the intrinsic of reality" (p. 96).

When the scientific method entered the world, claiming the potential of a more accurate method of discovery, the die was cast for an eventual reaction against it. Numerous scientific discoveries did, however, make positive changes to the challenges of survival through greater efficiency in agriculture, medicine, and industry.

It also created false hopes for the complete eradication of all issues detrimental to human life. The new science was thought to be a substitute for God. These assertions, in conjunction with the false outcomes they generated (such as illiteracy, poverty, and the elimination of wars), created moral objections that eventually led to the reactionary movement known as postmodernism.

Postmodernism became a blatant protest against the perfectionist promises of the early philosopher-scientists. It exposed the greed of the Enlightenment entrepreneurs, the atrocities toward workers during the Industrial Revolution, and the devastation of two world wars.

FALSE PROMISES EXPOSED:
EARLY PRECURSORS TO POSTMODERNISM

Enlightenment thinkers, wary of superstitions and rituals detrimental to the improvement of the human condition, sought to replace antiquated traditions with science and reason. Ignorance was believed to be a significant hindrance to the progress that modernist thinkers sought to overcome.

The development of the powers of rationalist logic, in the form of the scientific method and its various discoveries, sought to improve the world through the forces of intellect, empiricism (objective evaluation), human productivity, and individual endeavor. Hicks (2011) states that "reason [is] the means by which individuals can come to know their world, plan their lives, and interact socially" (p. 23).

The Enlightenment (movement toward the light) was paradoxical. It contained a positive side and a negative side. The positive side emphasized new interest in books, book clubs, journals, education, and the cognitive aspects of the universe.

The glass industry made a significant contribution with the production of telescopes, microscopes, and eyeglasses. Newly acquired knowledge set the pace for an agenda of change. Jacob (2001) discusses the philosophical beliefs of Immanuel Kant, who embraced the Enlightenment. It was Kant's belief that individuals should use their own understanding. He believed that this was the foundation of the Enlightenment.

Enlightenment thinkers were characterized by an unwavering commitment to science and its narrow path to truth. Information alone, devoid of any physical proof, was not taken seriously, which weakened the time-honored tenets of religion. Especially discouraging to religious adherents was the dismissal of faith principles, the authority of scripture, and the authenticity of prayer.

The Enlightenment prototype was emotionally mature, educationally advanced, culturally experienced, and skillfully involved in business and industry. The model of the Enlightenment individual was one who was married with well-educated children who excelled their various academic pursuits. Turning ordinary objects into profitable commodities was a family strategy that would provide generational wealth. Individuals pursuing medical endeavors would find cures to devastating diseases just as scientific invention would develop efficient industrial equipment. Attendees at a social event hosted by Thomas Jefferson are described by Ambrose (1998): "whether from Europe or America, they were men of the enlightenment, well-educated, intensely curious, avid readers and pursuers of new knowledge . . . about natural history and geography" (p. 34).

In many ways, the Enlightenment was a disguised form of intellectual and material perfectionism. Enlightenment thinkers believed that scientific invention and industrial competition, when energized by rugged individualism, would completely extinguish poverty and its causes. The mass production of material goods would produce wealth and power, which in turn would engender medical science with the ability to solve the mysteries of sickness and disease.

Class distinctions would also fade as a result of the potential for individuals to shape their lives as they saw fit. Enlightenment intellectuals believed that when the doors of opportunity were opened, the distribution of goods, combined with the intellectual emphasis on reason, would universally bind people together. The common goal of attaining increased knowledge and a more comfortable lifestyle would also be a potent motivational force for world peace.

Protests from the Romantic Era Philosophers and Poets

Philosophers of the Romantic era were the first to take issue with the intractable empiricism of the Enlightenment scientists. They were early precursors of the postmodern movement, protesting with poems and other writings. From the perspective of Romanticism, the Enlightenment belief system blocked the interplay of emotions, creativity, and experience. Romanticism spanned approximately one hundred years beginning in the 1770s in Europe culminating in the1870s in the United States.

Scientific objectivity reduced the individual to a thinking machine. Therefore, it was important to show the uniqueness of human existence by exhibiting the innate attributes of imagination, feelings, and freedom of the will. Scottish philosopher David Hume (1888) wrote, "No quality of human nature is more remarkable, both in itself and in its consequences, than that propensity we have to sympathize with others, and to receive, by communication, their inclinations and sentiments, however different from, or even contrary to, our own" (p. 225).

Notable historical figures—Jean-Jacques Rousseau, Ralph Waldo Emerson, Henry David Thoreau, William Wordsworth, and Walt Whitman among them—criticized the absolutism of the scientific method, firmly holding to the belief that the universe could never be precisely measured.

Rousseau, one of the outspoken fathers of Romanticism, took issue with Enlightenment thinkers about mankind becoming equals with one another through reason alone. Rousseau (2011) wrote that "inequality exists in the different privileges enjoyed by some at the expense of others, such as being richer, more honored, more powerful than they, or even causing themselves to be obeyed by them."

Emerson—minster, poet, philosopher, and leader of the transcendentalist movement—viewed the world as separate entities composed of sun, moon, animal, and tree. He defied the philosopher-scientists when he put the soul of man as foremost. Since the soul was not quantifiable using the scientific method, Enlightenment scientists believed that it served no useful purpose. Emerson (2010) wrote, "Nature hates calculators; her methods are salutatory and impulsive" (p. 99). Emerson maintained that most things are related to God and therefore most things are divine: "Meantime within man is the soul of the whole; the wise silence; the universal beauty, to which every art and particle is related, the eternal ONE" (p. 56).

Thoreau—environmentalist, philosopher, and poet—communicated and wrote extensively on the joy and challenge, beyond scientific findings, of living in the world as a human being. About scientific inquiries, he wrote that scientific investigations run the risk of being "trivial and petty," so perhaps what one should do is "learn science and then forget it" (Furtak 2019). When comparing the objectivity of science and the subjectivity of humanness, he states that it may be "impossible for the same person to see things from the poet's point of view and that of the man of science" (Furtak 2019).

In contrast to the unwavering Enlightenment belief in objectivity, subjectivity and emotions were at the core of the Romantic movement. By sharing and understanding the inner life, the Romantics believed they could bring their readers to a new understanding of life, love, and the struggles of ordinary people. Imagination and creativity were seen as equal to scientific rationality, and the way in which reality is perceived was a dominant theme.

Wordsworth (1994), a featured poet of the Romantic period, believed that poetry had a great deal to do with spontaneous feelings. His viewpoint emphasized a significant turning point in literary history. Wordsworth was profoundly affected by landscape, which he credited for his imagination and love of nature. His descriptive use of language enticed readers into their own experiences. The strict objectivity of the philosopher-scientists was replaced by subjective verbal descriptions. Wordsworth wrote, "rocks that muttered . . . crags that spake . . . voices were in them" (p. 813).

Whitman (2005), America's poet, revealed a divine imagination using emblematic language. He frequently described ordinary items commonly found in nature: ants, heap'd stones, poke-weed, and grass. Whitman believed that nature served a divine purpose. Refusing to accept the Enlightenment's perspective about a godless world, he personalized God with a strong belief that God is at the center of everything.

In contrast to the strict objectivity of the Enlightenment scholars, Romantic era philosophers supported feelings, emotions, experience, subjective interpretations, and the notion of a soul. Nature was a primary source for grasping these entities. The development of self was also a continuous theme to the Romantics.

Protests from the Romantic Era Philosophers and Novelists

Novels serve many useful purposes. They expose false promises, influence new ways of acquiring knowledge, create feelings, and construct new values to replace the antiquated ones of previous generations. Personal narratives create experiential reality in life challenges, cultural stories uncover bigotry, and stories of resistance expose corruption and greed. Currie (1998) states that "it [is] more than descriptive power . . . the way that fiction can position us, can manipulate our sympathies, can pull our heart strings, in the service of some moral aim" (p. 18).

The prediction of the Enlightenment with regard to a scientifically driven perfect society did not happen. It took exposure through novels, based on historical events, to show the reading public that the responsibility to change dire circumstances could come only from people themselves. Children could be conduits for change along with adults. Novels were also important in pointing out future dilemmas.

Objection against the mistreatment of factory workers is the theme of Charles Dickens's *Oliver Twist.* Upton Sinclair's *The Jungle* sheds light the unsafe working conditions in Chicago meatpacking plants as well as on the unhealthy meat sold to the public. Isolation created by war is witnessed in Erich Maria Remarque's *All Quiet on the Western Front.* John Steinbeck's iconic novel *The Grapes of Wrath* dismisses the Enlightenment principle of rugged individualism. The objectification of Holocaust statistics while overlooking the stories behind them is depicted in *Night* by Elie Wiesel. Resistance toward traditional values is portrayed by John Updike in *Rabbit, Run.* Prejudice revealed in racism, classism, and sexism dominate the small town of Maycomb in the popular novel *To Kill a Mockingbird* by Harper Lee.

Loss of Human Dignity

The strengths of the Industrial Revolution soon developed into glaring weaknesses. One example was the loss of human dignity. Early novels were entirely devoted to children trapped in difficult working circumstances.

The Charles Dickens character Oliver Twist coped with the horrors of the trade of chimney sweeping. In this classic novel, Dickens ruminates upon his own excruciating experiences while working at Warren's Blacking Factory at the age of twelve. His father was in debtors' prison at the time.

Contrary to the promises of the Enlightenment, poverty was widespread. Adults and children alike became a part of the product instead of the skilled workforce manufacturing the product. Dickens (1839, 2006) described the unending hours in rat-infested quarters and meager dispensation of food: "three meals of thin gruel a day, with an onion twice a week and half a roll-on Sunday" (p. 11).

President Theodore Roosevelt, sickened after reading an advance copy of Sinclair's *The Jungle* (1906), called upon Congress to pass the law that established the Food and Drug Administration. For the first time, federal inspectors set the standards for meatpacking industry, replacing corrupt inspectors who could be bribed. In the novel, Sinclair describes an inspector who was known for socialization instead of inspection: "If you were a sociable person, he was quite willing to enter conversation with you . . . and while talking with you . . . a dozen carcasses were passing him untouched" (p. 38).

Sinclair took direct aim at the Enlightenment. When jobs were difficult to find, workers were plentiful, driving wages down. The workers in city meatpacking plants often felt trapped, similar to the animals that were being slaughtered. Upward mobility was not possible. Wage increases were stunted due to the drive for higher profits. Absences because of illness were not tolerated, so only the fit survived. Abuse of alcohol was rampant due to the lack of hope inherent in poverty, and families lost the value of mutual cooperation that had been vital in the agrarian past.

The meatpacking industry, child labor, and the creation of machines that could replace workers were examples of the Industrial Revolution's insatiable desire to create wealth regardless of how it affected the labor force. "Wealth at all costs," regardless of safety standards that were violated, represents Truth (capital T). To postmodernists, it represents another example of the hollow promises of Enlightenment thinkers. The Enlightenment was predicted to end poverty, war etc. Part of the promise was greater wealth. Creating more wealth didn't always have any qualifiers (regulation) to it. Wealth, regardless of how it was accumulated, was foremost.

Isolation

Many high school and college students are familiar with Erich Maria Remarque's classic novel *All Quiet on the Western Front* (1929/1982), set largely in the trenches of Germany and France, referred to as "no man's land."

Desolation and carnage are witnessed in the descriptions of numerous burned-out villages. Years later, the soldiers who survived the ordeal of war would be described as a lost generation: "Now if we go back, we will be weary, broken, burnt out, rootless without hope. We will not be able to find our way anymore. And men will not understand us . . . and the Generation that has grown up after us will be strange to us and push us aside" (p. 294).

Memories often became demons that haunted the dreams of those who survived. For many, isolation and loss of identity were prevalent as they struggled to overcome horrid memories that prevented their reentry into society, creating isolated lifestyles. The introduction to the book states, "It will try to tell of a generation of men, who, even though they may have escaped shells, were destroyed by the war" (p. vi). The philosopher-scientist advocates of the Enlightenment were convinced that the new science would eliminate the need for war. They were sadly mistaken.

Rugged Individualism

Thinkers of the Enlightenment were supporters of individualism, emphasizing human autonomy as the principal strategy for achievement. An economic downturn of epic proportions and the advent of World War I quickly clouded the vision of individualism as the primary means of achievement. In order to endure the years from 1930 to 1945, Americans would be forced to pull together in a collective effort for survival.

On October 29, 1929, the day referred to as "Black Tuesday," the stock market crashed. During the decade that followed, vast numbers of people were abandoned by the banks they helped to build and, most disappointing of all, forgotten by the government that was the recipient of their loyalty. The majority of the population was forced to survive without ample food, shelter, and clothing. Homelessness was rampant as temporary relief was nonexistent.

Foreclosures on farms due to the Dust Bowl created mass movement of families across the country. Unfortunately, wives rarely worked for a salary, so the only funds available were those earned by men, who often left families destitute. Due to the inequity of unfair financial practices, the Great Depression became a time of extreme displacement.

When describing the Great Depression, Watkins (1993) writes, "I think there remains a powerful sense of connectedness, even among those

Americans that are comparatively young. Much of that connectedness can be attributed to the stories still told by so many people who survived those times and carry those memories with them. Passed on orally in many families . . ." (p. 7).

In his iconic book *The Grapes of Wrath* (1939), Steinbeck describes the hopelessness of people, specifically the farmers of this era. Steinbeck realistically emphasizes the themes of desperation and the need for new forms of community due to family migration. Rugged individualism, a motivational principle of the Enlightenment and the Industrial Revolution, was no longer possible. Community cooperation replaced it as a matter of sheer survival.

The story revolves around a tenant Oklahoma farming family, the Joads, who were evicted from their land. The tractor, invented during the Industrial Revolution, was able to do the work of several families; unfortunately, poor tenant farmers could not afford one. The banks, foreclosing on the Joad land (as well as that of many other farmers), used tractors to flatten the land, which included homes, barns, and other structures.

Ironically, the tractor's invention was designed to make farming significantly more productive and lucrative: "The iron guard . . . crumbled the wall. . . wrenched the little house. . . . [I]t fell sideways crushed like a bug" (p. 39).

Due to the devastation of the Dust Bowl, low profit margins, and the lack of efficient affordable machinery, farmers like the Joads were forced to travel to California in search of work. Steinbeck describes the grim, almost macabre, living conditions experienced by the Joad family as they make their trek to find work in California.

Throughout the novel, Steinbeck continues to build on the notion of community. Community becomes a place of security, belonging, cooperation, and contribution. Statements of unity are made by traveling migrants:

> In the evening a strange thing happened . . . the twenty families became one family; the children were the children of all. . . . We're proud to help. (p. 142–145)

> I ain't felt so safe in a long time . . . people needs to help. (p. 145)

> Each'll help each, an will all get to California. (p. 152)

> We gonna see you get through. . . . You said yourself. You can't let help go unwanted. (p. 153)

> Every night, relationships that make a world, established. (p. 200)

> A hungry man fed a hungry man, and then insured himself against hunger. (p. 202)

> Our people are good people; our people are kind people. Pray God someday a kid can eat. (p. 248)

If you're in trouble or hurt you need-go to poor people. They're the only ones
that'll help—the only ones. (p. 391)

Once again, the perfectionist arrogance of Enlightenment assurances fell
short. However, the postmodern concept of community construction was
born. As a result of the perils of migrant workers during the Great Depression, the colloquial phrase "I've got your back" gradually developed into a
cornerstone in the postmodern community.

The Holocaust

Statistics are objective sources of information and often seem cold and inani-
mate. Personal stories, however, retain the lifelike quality of past events. The
emotional impact of narratives are rarely erased from our memory. Personal
accounts often turn vicarious experiences into life-learning narratives for
personal and collective consequence.

The majority of the literature written about the horrid, evil incarceration
of the European Jewish people was authored in the post-Holocaust period. In
his moving novel *Night* (1958/2006), Wiesel turned statistics into a narrative
for all to experience, writing, "For the survivor . . . his duty is to bear witness
for the dead and for the living . . . to forget would be akin to killing them a
second time . . . memories will soon be lost. For in the end, it's all about
memory" (p. xv).

Elie Wiesel and his family were a part of a forced evacuation from their
home, city, and extended family. Wiesel was a teenager when the fascist
Hitler regime relocated them to Auschwitz and later to Buchenwald. In these
camps, he was confronted with the purest form of evil: beatings and even
death at the whim of those in charge, random evaluations to determine the
next person for the death chambers, babies tossed into the air for shooting
targets, and death marches between camps.

It was not Wiesel's intention to tell the story of his experiences to elicit
sympathy for the Jewish people, to hate those who joined the Nazi movement, or simply to depict a historical event. Rather, his personal story communicated the urgent need to view justice as an experience that turns to
action.

Traditional Values

World War II ended with ticker tape parades and historic adulation. The
Korean War finished in a stalemate. Soldiers were reunited with their families and a boom of babies was imminent. The world was safe for democracy—at least, that was the promise.

The Cold War began with *Sputnik*, the creation of nuclear weapons, and
the spread of communism. The spread of polio, which had been progressing

since the turn of the twentieth century, reached its peak in the United States in the 1950s, claiming thousands of lives and leaving countless others disabled. Jonas Salk's vaccine, introduced in 1955, halted the menace of polio, and hope among parents was restored.

This brief period of hope and prosperity was rudely interrupted by impending threats of nuclear annihilation and the stalemate of the Cold War. For some, this created a moral dilemma, and two choices became apparent: A person could choose to live in accordance with culture-proven traditional values, or one could oppose them, at least in the short term. For many, involuntary conscription to fight communist aggression in Vietnam solidified their choice as the latter of the two.

Updike foreshadowed the decade that would follow in his Pulitzer Prize–winning novel *Rabbit, Run* (1960). Updike's main character, Harry "Rabbit" Angstrom, is trapped in a life of monotony and mundane routine. Janice, Harry's pregnant wife, is an alcoholic. Nelson, the couple's first child, adds to the stress of family life as the parents lose freedom and flexibility. When Janice delivers their second child, they will have a typical American family. Harry, however, is bored and desires more. His job as a demonstrator of the revolutionary new MagiPeeler is devoid of any creativity or personal expression.

Harry feels trapped with limited escape routes: "[I]t seemed like I was glued in. Television going . . . meals late or never . . . no way of getting out" (p. 51). Harry's journey takes many twists and turns. He spends the entire novel running to catch the elusive answer to his existential journey for meaning within a changing society: "Then all of a sudden it hit me . . . just walk out . . . by dam it was easy" (p. 51).

After leaving his wife and son, Harry consults with his old basketball coach. The time-tested caricature of the coach is a person with traditional values: hard work, loyalty, and commitment to family values. Harry's idolized coach has also become a part of changing viewpoints. On the one hand, his former coach realizes the influence he possesses: "Give the boys the will to achieve. I've always liked that better than the will to win, for there can be achievement even in defeat . . . in the form of giving our best . . . a boy who had his heart enlarged by an inspiring coach . . . can never become, in the deepest sense, a failure in the greater game of life" (p. 105).

The irony of Coach Tothero's brief homily is that it is delivered in the presence of his prostitute friends, Margret and Ruth, whom he has introduced to Harry. Tothero does not exhort him to return to his wife or to remain true to his marriage vows; he simply tells Harry to "do what his heart commands. The heart is our only guide" (p. 62). Interestingly, Harry believes he has, in fact, followed his heart.

In an attempt to reconcile the paralyzing dualism of new freedom and traditional restrictions, Harry reluctantly spends more time with Ruth. He asks her a simple question: He wants to know why she likes him. Her answer is concise and to the point: "'Cause you haven't given up. In your stupid way, you're still fighting" (p. 53).

Essentially, Ruth communicates that she admires Harry because he represents a new and perhaps fresh protest against the traditional mantra that "you should, you must, you ought." She senses that Harry is on to something new and untried—namely, a viewpoint about life that differs from the universal truth scripts handed down from traditions of the past.

Harry experiences the challenge of maintaining the foundational ethic of his past at the birth of his daughter. Harry says, "Help me, Christ. Forgive me. Take me down the way" (p. 52). Harry, however, is well aware that he is going to leave Janice again. Later in the story, Janice goes on a drinking spree during which she accidentally drowns the new baby, Rebecca.

The vise squeezing Harry is the predictability of the consequences of traditional morality on the one hand, and the insatiable desire to break free from it on the other. The title for the first of the Rabbit novels is not random or accidental. Truly, Harry is running from what is known in conventional society to what is unknown. Fundamentally, he is running from traditional values. He runs from his wife, he runs to Ruth, and then he runs back to Janice at the birth of his daughter.

As the novel concludes, Rabbit is on the run again, this time after the funeral of baby Rebecca: "His hands lift of their own . . . he feels the wind on his ears . . . his heels hitting heavily on the pavement at first . . . with an effortless gathering out of a kind of sweet panic, growing lighter and quicker and quieter he runs. Ah: runs. Runs" (p. 308).

Bigotry and Prejudice

In *To Kill a Mockingbird,* prejudice runs rampant throughout the small town of Macomb, Alabama. Tom Robinson, a black man accused of raping Mayella Ewell, is the unquestionable victim of glaring bigotry. Even though Atticus Finch, the city attorney and the novel's depiction of moral clarity, clearly proves that Tom is innocent, he is convicted of the crime and is later shot and killed.

Mayella, the supposed victim, is only vaguely aware that the townspeople label her family "white trash." Her father, Bob Ewell, persecutes Tom as a strategy to elevate his own status and to cover up Mayella's own advances toward Tom.

Others in the community are subject to false judgment as well. Mrs. Dubose, who yells at Jem and Scout as they walk by is described as "the meanest old woman who ever lived" (p. 90). Most people are unaware of her morphine addiction and her insatiable desire to die on her terms. After her death she gains favor in the eyes of Jem and Scout as a brave individual.

When Aunt Alexandria comes to visit Jem, Scout, and Atticus, her immediate desire is to fire Calpurnia. Aunt Alexandria's motive has nothing to do with the work ethic of Calpurnia, who takes care of the children; rather, Aunt Alexandria must fire Calpurnia to show Jem and Scout the proper attitude toward heritage and class.

When Boo Radley, the town's recluse, emerges from the shadows, Jem and Scout begin to interact with him and discover that the cruel gossip about him is simply not true. But instead of attempting to reach out to him, the town had shunned him.

Jem and Scout are abruptly ushered out of innocence during the trial of Tom Robinson; the ugly racism of Macomb is pushed to the forefront as Tom is found guilty regardless of facts that show him to be innocent. Meanwhile, the false rumors about Boo Radley imprison him in a solitary life. Both characters illustrate the symbolism of the mockingbird.

The bigotry, generational sexism, and cruel, unfounded verbal mistruths describe the way life in Maycomb *is*. At the same time, Atticus and his ever-present kindness, fairness, and even pity for Mayella Ewell, personifies how it *could be*.

The postmodern movement challenged traditional viewpoints and birthed new ones. The rigid scientific truths of the Enlightenment surrendered to humanness. The result was increased equality, freedom of expression, and nuances of life that centered on the themes of acceptance and encouragement. As a result, children were able to begin participating co-equally with adults. More attention and financial resources were distributed, at least in suburban school budgets, to increase academic success among children. Various school districts created their own verbiage for identifying success: A+, "Best" school designations, failing schools, etc. It is not uncommon for school officials to give motivational speeches in an assembly empathizing the notion that "we are all in this together."

Gene Hackman's quote from the movie "Hoosiers" (Angelo Pizzo film, 1986), "Five players on the floor functioning as one single unit: team, team, team—no one more important than the other," is a foundational quote for the concept of co-equals. Some schools have it pinned to the hallway wall.

Chapter Three

Postmodern Children

Story Creators and Storytellers

"The spontaneous power of the child, his demand for self-expression, cannot by any possibility be suppressed." —John Dewey

Today's children believe that differing points of view can be valid. They are skeptical of stereotypes. Postmodern children have a comprehensive view of life, including a special sensitivity for what is known as the Other, a desire to live in harmony with nature, living cooperatively instead of competitively with others, respecting the wisdom and practices of all cultures, viewing the world as an organism rather than a machine, and people who might be challenged in their living situations.

Powell (1998) points out that the world is diminishing, and a dominant worldview no longer exists. Plurality exists all around us. The Other can refer to other individuals, groups, races, geographies, the conscious mind, rational mind, and even the outer or inner self. He emphasizes the idea that our world resists grand narratives even though certain individuals or groups desire them to continue. Reality, as it is experienced, is not as real as we once believed it to be and that our beliefs are not eternal but created; "our world is a carnival of colorful and contradictory worldviews" (p. 150–51).

EMPHASIS ON STORY (NARRATIVES)

Reality that is experienced in personal accounts is germane to children. Postmodern children love stories. Narratives are authentic accounts of survival in the greater community in which they live. They acquaint children with the cultures of other countries, reminding them that struggle is common to all.

Today's children learn to appreciate the uniqueness of other cultures and desire to hear community stories of life and survival. They are able to discern that most people are faced with challenging situations both similar to and vastly different from their own. The strategies used by other people to solve problems are educational to them. As Brandt (1997) notes, "Story, then, is not just a frill, an illustration, a diversion, or an entertainment, as the modern scientific mindset maintained. Instead, story is much more basic. It is a way by which and through which we come to understand ourselves, others, the world around us" (p. viii).

From the unique challenges of early life on the prairie to the complicated challenges in suburban and city life, children are amazingly capable. The following are a small sampling of those stories. The stories have transpired in the recent past, but they continue to show the incredible courage, compassion and creativity of children. National news continues to cover positive acts of young people.

THE OTHER

A common theme in postmodern thought revolves around the term *Otherness*. Characteristic of postmodern intelligence is an array of definitions that adhere to a single term. Otherness is no exception. According to Esteva and Prakash (1998), postmodernism embraces cultural differences and seeks to encourage "non-modern majorities into opportunities for regenerating their own traditions, their cultures, and their unique indigenous and other non-modern arts of living and dying" (p. 5).

The children in the following story clearly embraced cultural differences. They accepted children from a different culture and were helpful to them in their transition. Their countries of origin were completely different, but they learned from each other. Fellow classmates even learned some new soccer skills. Postmodern children do this almost instinctively.

EXPERIENCING A CULTURE OF THE OTHER

A Brief Story from the Lives of Albanian Children

A few years ago, I visited with an elementary school teacher who taught in the inner city. It was shortly after the Kosovo War.

> We had an influx of children from Albania. Most of the children had very little exposure to the English language. We accepted their native tongue, knowing that eventually they would learn English because the teachers taught in English. We allowed the children to come to class and simply observe what we were teaching. We graded them in narrative form with two or three paragraphs

about their progress. It was not the school district's intention to pressure them into an instantaneous grasp of English through tutors or small groups. The district also allowed them to speak to one another at lunch and recess in their own language.

Teachers allowed them some latitude in classroom behavior when it was obvious they were "bored out of their minds" because they had no idea what was being taught. By March, the children knew enough English to participate in all that the class was doing. The most effective tutoring came from the other children in the class. In my mind, they were the educators and the teachers. The Albanian children were an instant success at recess because of their soccer skills. Everyone learned a great deal about the value of respect. (Personal interview)

Children are capable!

It is not difficult to imagine the important role that both the English-speaking children and the Albanian children could play in a school district's approach to immigrant children. Both groups of students could be given a voice of importance, providing new insights into the early American experience. Teachers, school district officials, parent meetings and journalists could benefit from their presentations.

Modernism promised to overcome human differences by providing a universal viewpoint. Modern thinkers postulated that cultures developed out of ancient, nonscientific traditions and would naturally unite under the banner of reason. Postmodernism views world culture differently, giving credence to emotions, subjectivity, and varied interpretations. Since postmodern children are exposed to a plurality of traditions, they naturally acquire a spirit of equality with regard to dignity and respect for others.

Students realize, largely through exposure and experience, that cultures are often mislabeled. Discussing cultural labels or any other universal definitions, Brown (2005) states, "Postmodernism denies that it is impossible to show reality, only versions of it. . . . Nobody can know everything about a subject, and there is *never* only one authority on a given subject." Brown goes on to say that a personal account—or any other account—is "contingent (upon new knowledge) and temporary" (p. 7).

Observation, exposure, and experience with a plurality of people who might be disrespected by fixed norms in a society can also be a motivation for today's children to vote in both local and national elections when they are eligible.

Immigration issues can dominate the political discussion, at times with very little progress. Exposure to the Other enhances children's development of worldview. Giving children a voice of importance when they are young will undoubtedly prompt them to verbalize their viewpoints in other settings when they are older.

THE STORY OF A CHILD TRAPPED IN
THE MARGINALIZED OTHER

A Brief Story from the Life of Jezebel

The Other also refers to individuals or groups of people who are marginalized or overlooked. It includes people who are poor, uneducated, or mired in a manner of living that keeps them in paralyzing circumstances. Geography, unjust political and educational systems, meager wages, and inequality of opportunity are usually the precursors. Sometimes the marginalized Other is closer to everyday life than is realized. Today's children are acutely aware of these conditions.

Urban school districts have historically fallen into the marginalized category. Kozol (1991) describes the marginalized Other in the circular nature of opportunity for children, depending on where they live. Richer school districts with higher property values acquire more tax dollars to fund their public schools. Therefore, they are able to hire enough teachers to lower the class sizes. They are also able to purchase newer textbooks and lab equipment. The distinction of a particular school becomes known by increasing land and home prices, which results in a higher tax base to fund the schools.

Says Jezebel:

> I have a friend who is in the eleventh grade. She goes to school in Cherry Hill. I go to her house, and I compare the work she's doing with the work I'm doing. In each class at her school in Cherry Hill, they have the books they're supposed to for their grade levels. Here, I'm in the eleventh grade. I take American history. I have an eighth-grade book. So, I have to ask, "Well, are they three years smarter? Am I stupid?" But it's not like that at all. Because we're kids like they are. We're no different. And, you know, there are smart people here. But then, you know, they have the money goin' to their schools. They have a nice clean school to go to. They have carpets on the floors and air-conditioned rooms and brand-new books. Their old books, when they're done with them, they ship them here to us. . . . [W]hat I want to know is this: Why are the levels of our work so different? What we call a C at our school is a D in Cherry Hill. And I'm thinking, "I can *get* it. I can work at my grade level same as them. Maybe better. I can do as well as others." (Kozol, p. 152)

Jezebel has a keen understanding of the marginalized Other and displays a respectable spirit of protest. She experiences, in real time, what it means to be left out based entirely on where she lives. Jezebel believes in her ability to perform at the same level as her friend; however, she has a formidable obstacle to overcome simply due to her school's budget for grade-level books. She is clearly marginalized by her school circumstances. The postmodern principle of equality is foremost on her mind.

Perhaps the most challenging task for Jezebel is to overcome a perceived feeling of less-than based entirely on the financial circumstances of her particular school district. Jezebel shows keen insights into the politics of the rich and the poor in school district politics. She is forced to use textbooks that are subpar even though her potential for intellectual achievement is the same, perhaps even greater.

Jezebel and her classmates could be given a voice of importance that influences policymakers at the district, state, and even national levels. The equal distribution of funds is challenging in any state.

THE EXPERIENCE OF A CHILD LIVING
AS THE DISRESPECTED OTHER

A Story of Living in Affordable Housing

Another aspect of Otherness centers on the necessity of dignity for all people as they live in their respective cultures. Respect for culture gives authenticity to the idea that other societies view life tasks from different perspectives.

Matters of life, death, religious beliefs, and family values can vary from country to country and village to village. Esteva and Prakash (1998) define what they call political humility. They write, "Political humility struggles for the dignity of all peoples, embracing the premise which rejects the supposed superiority of any culture, any ideology, any political position, over the others. It dreams of a world in which everyone can pose and propose their views and intentions to others, but no one can impose their own on others" (p. 202).

The next story reveals the discouragement of a girl living in affordable housing. She was often viewed by others in judgmental ways. Unfortunately, income labeling by others seemed like an unbreakable chain. Regardless of academic or athletic achievements, unfounded opinions by students and parents remained in place. Influenced by postmodernity, she knew her living arrangements could be seen in a more positive way.

My family and I grew up in an area where trailers were commonplace. We just couldn't afford anything else. It wasn't always that way. My dad was in a serious car accident and became disabled. My mom did the best she could working for a restaurant cleanup crew. As soon as my brothers and sisters were old enough to work, we found jobs.

We were on the receiving end of a countless number of names: irresponsible, poor, disgraceful, uneducated, and trailer trash. Very few of us could participate in sports due to our workloads. One kid, however, had more talent in basketball than others in the trailer park. We lived about two miles from the school. He rode his bike to the school as often as possible with his basketball in his hand.

My brother was outstanding in math. His grades were remarkable, and he happened to be the same age as the neighbor who was talented in basketball. Even though they both gained notoriety in the school community, they were still known as the kids from the trailer park. We were disrespected for as long as we lived there. I made the decision to do something about it as an adult.

Eventually, I became a teacher and specifically looked for a district with a significant population of students from affordable housing situations. I petitioned and was granted the opportunity to teach a class about the acceptance of others regardless of their living conditions. It helped the students in their inclusion skills, and it helped me overcome the labels from my past. (Personal interview)

Most suburban or semi-suburban school districts have older neighborhoods that are composed of duplexes or other affordable housing units. The acute feelings of anxiety each day must have been unimaginable. How does a young student overcome such a stigma?

Each morning, when schoolchildren emerge from their homes, all their peers on the school bus can see the type of house they live in, and each evening they return. Parents of children who live in better living situations might caution their children about playing with classmates from the affordable housing projects. Acceptance based on commonality of going to the same school would likely be nonexistent. For many of these children, developing and maintaining a recognized social life may seem impossible.

Similar to the aforementioned story, a voice of importance could be given about the experience of living under many negative labels. Children living in the affordable housing areas could speak to parents or write articles in the local newspaper explaining how it feels to be labeled and the resulting discouragement.

THE DISREGARDED (FORGOTTEN) OTHER

Families living in the suburbs are often surprised by the high truancy rates in the inner city due to the obstacles students have to overcome in order to attend school. Once truancy begins, it usually increases at an alarming rate. Very few people grasp the never-ending challenges involved with living in the inner city. Children who struggle on a daily basis feel unnoticed and forgotten.

A Brief Story from the Life of Billie

Children living in discouraging circumstances present a challenging scenario. Students skip school for a variety of reasons, from preparing for prom night to simply taking a "mental health day." But for those who usually reside in pockets of poverty in the city, lack of interest influences student truancy, as does substance abuse, criminal activity, and gang membership. Truancy, with a pattern of missed days and weeks, leaves the child vulnerable to dropping out altogether.

In "Habits Hard to Break," Roderick (1997) relates a story about the challenges of a student named Billie:

> Billie, an African American adolescent, was in trouble in the eighth grade. She had been in the same elementary school since kindergarten but generally had low skills. Largely unsupervised at home and wanting for money, Billie had spotty eighth grade attendance. In the middle of the eighth grade, she was transferred to another classroom. It was a transfer she had difficulty handling academically and socially. She coped with her problems by hanging out in an alley near school with much older boys. Billie's first homeroom teacher was a key support. Her teacher got her reenrolled in school, often bought her meals, and gave her attention. *"She bought me clothes, she bought me something for Christmas. . . . and if I had trouble with my work, she spent like, extra time on me and stuff."*
>
> Over the summer, Billie's home situation unraveled. Her mom lost custody, and Billie moved in with a sister in the suburbs. This arrangement didn't work. Billie bounced from relative to relative. She lived with an aunt until she got *"put out."* Her father gained custody but also appeared to be struggling with debt and homelessness. Billie's school address listed her father and her as residing in a relative's nursing home room. She supported herself by selling drugs. For example, Billie explained that she needed a uniform to enroll in school. *" 'Cause I couldn't come to school 'cause my daddy ain't buy me what I need."* When asked how she was finally able to purchase a uniform, she answered, *"I bought it. . . I just got it selling drugs."*
>
> She enrolled in high school in October, *"because I need to come to school. . . . Ain't nobody going to hire me without no high school education. . . cause I want a job and my own apartment so I can get away from everybody."* She spent little time in her classes, finding refuge in the social worker's office. By winter, Billie stopped coming to school. The relative died and the father left no forwarding address. For several months, Billie's mother and uncle claimed not to know Billie's whereabouts. By spring she enrolled in the Job Corps, in a facility outside Chicago where she continued to work toward finishing high school. Had Billie not enrolled in an alternative program and found this stable environment, her path might have continued downhill. (p. 6)

Billie could have easily become a girl of the streets—dealing drugs, entering the sex trade, or both. But somehow, a still small voice reverberated in her heart to keep fighting, to never give up, and to continue to come back to an educational setting. With a maturity beyond her years, she realized that she only had one option: She had to learn a marketable trade.

Billie could be given a voice of importance speaking to a parent group or school board, explaining the challenges of growing up without a stable family, the difficulties involved in finding a job, and the lure to sell drugs to earn money. Billie would do quite well in a question-and-answer forum. Children are capable!

STORIES SHOWING THE CAPABILITIES OF CHILDREN THROUGHOUT HISTORY

In every historical era, children have proved to be dependable, skillful, and committed in situations in which they were asked to contribute. The results of their involvement were remarkable.

FRONTIER LIFE

A Brief Story from the Life of Ulysses S. Grant

Fass (2016) reveals the historical importance of children in the struggle for family survival. Ulysses S. Grant, known for his Civil War successes as well as becoming the eighteenth president of the United States, was in charge of procuring wood for the house and shops. He also completed the farm work that was done with a plow.

> "When about 11 years old, I was strong enough to hold a plow. From that age until 17 I did all the work done with horses, such as breaking up the land, furrowing, plowing corn and potatoes, bringing in the crops when harvested, hauling all the wood, besides tending two or three horses, a cow or two and sawing wood for stoves, etc., while attending school." As he did almost all tasks of farming, young Ulysses was playing a significant part in the affairs of the Grant household.
>
> Grant's early life reflected the fact that he knew his part was important and valuable. In a relatively short period of time, he would assume a role on the world stage.'
>
> He explained that since he did everything expected of him, he was never scolded or punished, but was given the right to both 'rational enjoyments' and a large degree of independence. This independence allowed him to roam freely and travel widely, often for many miles beyond the family home and frequently overnight, even as a 10-year-old boy. He was allowed to trade horses (not always successfully) on his own account. (Fass, 2016, pp. 20–21)

THE CIVIL WAR

A Brief Story from the Life of Johnny Clem

Ohio History Central tells the story of Johnny Clem:

Johnny Clem was a soldier in the service of the United States for most of his life. He was born on August 13, 1851, in Newark, Ohio. His actual name was John Joseph Clem. Although Clem was only ten years old when the American Civil War began, he immediately tried to enlist in the Union Army.

Clem was one of ten thousand boys under the age of eighteen who served in the Union Army.

Soldiers provided him a gun and uniform and trained him to be a drummer boy. Clem was finally allowed to enlist in the United States Army in May 1863, when he was only twelve. In the meantime, Clem had already participated in numerous battles and had become quite famous.

According to most sources, at the Battle of Shiloh, Clem demonstrated his calmness under fire. A confederate cannonball supposedly smashed Clem's drum while the boy was playing it. His reputation grew more with his exploits at the Battle of Chickamauga. Confederate forces drove General William Rosecrans' Army of the Cumberland from the field. During the retreat, a Confederate colonel captured them, but Clem managed to escape by shooting the attacker. . . . Union journalists reported Clem's adventures to their readers. The drummer boy became an instant celebrity and earned nicknames like "Johnny Shiloh" and "The Drummer Boy of Chickamauga." For his bravery at Chickamauga, Clem was promoted to the rank of lance corporal. (Ohio History Central)

Clem changed his name to John Lincoln Clem and remained in the army, serving nearly fifty years through three wars. When he retired in 1916, he was the last of the Civil War veterans.

THE INDUSTRIAL REVOLUTION

Trattner (1970) gives historical perspective to the capabilities of children. Children were always incorporated into the life and survival of early communities. They hunted, fished, and trapped and also worked in other situations. When clans became families, they continued to toil, clearing forests, tilling fields, and taking care of animals. Trattner describes the Industrial Revolution as a reprehensible era where the selfish needs of factories manipulated children into service. Because children developed the aforementioned skills, they were easy prey to work in factories where safety was an ever-present danger.

Hindman (2002) sheds light on the importance of children to the labor force. Children were a source of cheap labor and could also be taught needed skills for profit in business and industry. Children were important to factories that specialized in consumer products, including pottery, furniture, brooms, and machine shop products.

Children were diligent workers in spite of their displacement: "With industrialization, poor children and their families were drawn off the family farm, out of the home workshop, or out of the urban tenement, into the mines, mills, and factories. . . . Several industries became dependent on child labor" (p. 5). The use of children for industrial profit, although egregious, revealed the capabilities of children!

Mullenbach (2014) builds on the themes of displacement, maturity, and the capabilities of children at a young age. After the death of her father, eight-year-old Lucy Larcom, along with her mother and siblings, moved from Beverly, Massachusetts, to Lowell, Massachusetts. Her mother found employment running a boarding house for workers at the Lawrence Manufacturing Company: "I thought it would be a pleasure to feel I was not a trouble or burden or expense to anybody. . . . [I]t really was not hard, just to change the bobbins of the spinning frames every three quarters of an hour or so, with half a dozen other little girls who were doing the same thing" (p. ix–xi).

THE STORY OF THE NEW ENGLAND MILL GIRLS

A story written by Bortoletti (1999) points out the role that child workers played in exposing their working conditions:

> The New England mill girls insisted they were the social and intellectual equal of men and well-to-do girls who didn't work. In their "improvement circles," they produced stories, poems and essays. With help from local clergy and mill owners, they published factory magazines such as *Lowell Offering* and *Factory Life*. *Lowell Offering* attracted national and international interest, as the girls received praise for their writing.
>
> In the beginning, the girls used the magazines to show that mill girls were intelligent and capable of producing thoughtful work. However, as conditions worsened and salaries failed to rise, the girls used the magazines to reveal the unpleasant side of factory life—situations owners wanted to keep hidden.
>
> The girls wrote stories that told of unbearable working conditions and the "evils of factory life." In their essays, the girls complained that the long hours left no time to cultivate the mind and form good habits. They wrote letters that told about overseers who took advantage of female workers, forcing the girls to "abandon virtue to obtain favors."
>
> Other girls complained about the poor wages and compulsory church attendance. "Here I am, a healthy New England girl, quite well behaved, bestowing just half of all my hours, including Sundays, upon a company for less than two cents an hour, and out of the other half of my time, I am obliged to wash, mend, read, reflect, go to church!! . . . What are we coming to?"
>
> As people read the magazines, they began to sympathize with girls about the working conditions: the long hours, low pay, and limited leisure time. The pubic began to criticize factory owners and their exploitation of factory labor.

There was no sadder sight, said some critics, than the thousands of mill girls on their way to and from work. Furthermore, some men decided that factory work ruined the health and reputations of even the worthiest and most virtuous girl. (p. 31–32)

THE GREAT DEPRESSION

Mullenbach (2015) describes the poverty, displacement, and hopelessness of the Great Depression. Many families were forced to migrate to locations where temporary work existed.

A now-famous spontaneous snapshot of a migrant mother and her children caught the attention of Americans across the country. The tension wrinkles on her face and the children, with their faces turned away from the camera, were notable.

> Long after the Great Depression ended, this image . . . symbolized the hopelessness of the time. School textbooks tried to describe the era.
>
> People who lived through it struggled to explain their feelings. But all anyone has to do is look into the face of the mother in the photograph to understand what it must have been like for many Americans during this time. . . . While shame and despair were widespread during those troubling times, many people who lived through the Great Depression recall other more positive memories: acts of courage, pride, and generosity shown by countless individuals and agencies. (p. xii)

The introduction of child stars to the public eye provided a brief respite to this era of depression: "A bunch of poor kids with memorable names—Spanky, Alfalfa, Buckwheat, and Porky—captured moviegoers of all ages in the 1930s. The 'Our Gang' series of short films began as silent productions in the 1920s. The actors who portrayed the kids changed over the years, but enthusiasm for the series prevailed" (p. 92–97). Another child star, Jackie Cooper, starred in the short films *Teacher's Pet*, *School's Out*, and *Love Business*.

The child actress who kidnapped the hearts and minds of all listeners was Shirley Temple: "One of the acts is a musical number by a six-year-old newcomer named Shirley Temple. 'Baby, Take a Bow' was a peppy performance audiences loved. . . . President Franklin Roosevelt said, 'As long as our country has Shirley Temple, we will be alright'" (92–97). Children are capable!

Chapter 3

THE CIVIL RIGHTS MOVEMENT

A Brief Story from the Life of Ruby Bridges

The civil rights movement spawned myriad stories revealing the commitment and capabilities of children. Many African American children, like their parents, were tired of being treated unfairly. Turck (2000) tells the following story about children and their participation in the civil rights movement:

> Ruby Bridges, age 6, was the first black child to attend a previously all-white school in New Orleans in 1960. Four federal marshals came to take Bridges to school that day. They walked Bridges through the crowds of white men and women.
>
> Grown men and women threw things and screamed insults as Bridges walked through the mob of people. She was not hit by any of the things they threw. Inside the school, she found herself in a classroom all alone with a teacher. All the white parents had kept their children home from school. Only one teacher, a woman who had just arrived from Boston, agreed to teach Bridges. (p. 12)

The four federal marshals were present every day. "Two, four, six, eight, we don't want to integrate" was chanted in hateful voices by the white adults. Some of the parents were so angry about integration they refused to allow their children to return to school for more than a year. Slowly, however, the white children went back to school. Eventually, Bridge's classroom filled up with students instead of empty desks. The parents wisely made the decision that "education was more important than segregation" (11–12).

As a parent with four children, Ruby Bridges Hall continues to work for education, children, and families. She tells people, "It is now a time for us to be concerned with all children, not just our own" (13).

Levine (1993) relates another story about a child during the civil rights movement: "Arlem was 5 years old when the bus boycott began. His mother had helped to organize the MIA [Montgomery Improvement Association], and so he understood what was happening. 'If I we were driving and I'd see somebody walking, I'd say, Mama, pick those people up!' When he reached high school age, he brought a lawsuit to end segregation in the Montgomery school system" (p. 148).

Discussing another incident during the civil rights movement, Matthews (2017) writes,

> In a new demonstration on May 2, hundreds of schoolchildren, then thousands of local school children, trained in the same civil disobedience, poured from the 16th Street Baptist Church, parading through the city again without a permit. . . .

The police met the oncoming crowd, some not yet teenagers, with high-pressure fire hoses. Though terrified, the young marchers kept singing as armed men with billy clubs bore down on them. . . . Twelve hundred children of various ages were now packed into jails meant to accommodate nine hundred. (p. 238–39)

Each fall, children everywhere make the trek to their first day of school. Depending on the child's previous experiences, his or her confidence may be challenged. Many children are anxious. As the day unfolds, uncontrollable events can happen. Groups are formed, seating locations are randomly assigned, discipline is meted out, and placement tests are administered whose results that might affect the label a child is given. All of these factors create stress.

In the civil rights era, one more stressor was added: angry adults screaming and chanting with hate emanating from their faces and the threat of harm resounding in their voices. Children are not only capable, they are also courageous.

THE PRESENT DAY

A Brief Story from the Life of Jaden and His Grandmother

Children continue to demonstrate courageous behavior beyond what we would expect. It is often difficult to comprehend how much they can contribute. Newscasts and newspapers often cite the heroic efforts of children in crisis situations.

Jaden's story was highlighted in newspapers and television news broadcasts:

Three-year-old Jaden Bolli, who lives in Maple Shade, NJ, was with his grandmother last Friday when she passed out. Knowing something was wrong, Bolli did what his mother told him to do just days before—he called 911.

The dispatcher asked him what the emergency was, and the toddler responded, "Mom-Mom's sick." Bolli's mother, Candace Robbins, just four days before the emergency instructed her son, "If you don't hear my heartbeat or somebody falls or anything, you have to dial 911, hit the green button and just tell them you need help." Bolli told Rodriguez [the interviewer] when his grandma fell down, "I called the cops." Rodriguez remarked that it's incredible he was able to stay so calm and call for help.

Early Show coanchor Maggie Rodriguez said, "Bolli told the dispatcher the emergency was his grandmother's blood sugar, but as it turns out, she'd had a stroke. Paramedics arrived just in time. Bolli's grandmother is in stable condition." CBS News medical correspondent Dr. Jennifer Ashton agreed, saying, "It's hard enough for adults to keep their composure in an emergency. . . . Bolli is a role model for children and adults alike" (Rodriguez & Ashton, 2010).

A Brief Story from the Life of Keegan and a Homeless Community

"In Eugene, Oregon, a ten-year-old boy battling cancer, decided to feed the homeless. It was on his bucket list. His parents are both unemployed. Keegan Keppner knows the challenges of overcoming adversity. He was fighting a rare form of brain cancer, which requires numerous cycles of chemotherapy."

Keegan has a heart for the homeless. The city of Eugene was closing a camping area where homeless people congregated. "'It's sad to see them suffer,' Keegan, a fourth-grade math whiz, told ABCNews.com. 'There are a lot of nice people down there'" (James, 2014).

Even though his parents struggled to make ends meet, Keegan convinced them to do what they could. So Keegan and his stepfather, Steven Macgray, decided to cook up a pot of rice and beans and take it down to the eighteen or so homeless people at the camping area. Keegan told his parents he wanted to give up Christmas dinner to feed them.

Keegan could be given a voice of importance. He could participate on a school district committee making decisions about efficiently distributing breakfast and hot lunch programs. If his school is allowed to participate with the homeless, Keegan would be very helpful. Keegan is protesting hunger. Sadly, Keegan lost his battle with cancer, but his actions were a catalyst for his parents and others to participate in his cause.

A Brief Story from the Lives of Kenneth and His Grandfather

NBC News (2016) reports the story of an invention by a teenager: Kenneth Shinozuka, an eleventh-grade student, has a desire to cure Alzheimer's disease. He hasn't graduated from medical school, but has invented a useful device. "I made this sock [speaking to one of the residents at a memory care facility] that lets Conrad [her care worker] know when you walk off your chair or out of bed, and lets him know if you need help." (Qtd. in NBC News, 2016)

The sock works off a sensor that Kenneth invented to detect an increase in pressure. It is worn on the bottom of the foot under a sock. When the sensor detects more pressure, it sends a warning signal to a caregiver's smart phone. The entire creation was initiated by Kenneth from scratch. It was essentially a self-taught exercise.

The idea came from experiences with his grandfather who was diagnosed with Alzheimer's disease when Kenneth was 4 years old and would often wander from his bed. In the first six months, the device, called the "Safe Wanderer," recorded 437 instances of unattended meandering.

"'I'd like to solve some of the mysteries of the brain and invent tools to ultimately, I think, cure Alzheimer's and other mental conditions that our aging population suffers from,' says Shinozuka." (NBC News, 2016).

Kenneth is protesting mental diseases. Kevin could be given a voice of importance about the need for innovative devices to help the aged. He is already active in science clubs and fairs. Perhaps he could get permission to speak in a large group forum at his high school and others in the district to share his vision in an attempt to motivate, inspire, and possibly recruit others to help with Alzheimer's disease. Children are capable!

A Brief Story from the Life of a Newly Hired Football Coach

Most (but certainly not all) assistant coaches, in any sport have a desire to be head coach. In order for this to happen, the principal and the athletic director need to be impressed with the assistant coaches current performance in both practices and in games. The following is a brief story about a coach who needed to show that, more often than not, he could handle challenging situations.

> I was hired as the new assistant head football coach. Needless to say, I was filled with hopes, dreams and visions. The first year, my greatest frustration occurred during the practices. I had no idea how difficult it would be to get the kids from one station to the next. I yelled, screamed, and threatened. Finally, I grabbed two of the biggest players and asked them to get the players from one place to the next. The two players came through, and the difficulty ceased. (Personal interview)

A Brief Story from the Life of a Teacher with a Broken Arm

Preparation is helpful to both the students and the teacher. Before the school year begins, teachers are busy organizing desks, arranging bulletin boards, and creating a room that is welcoming. Most veteran teachers handle the work as if it were second nature to them.

A teacher with a broken arm has a distinct disadvantage; they only have one arm to work with. Some instructors can still work on curriculum design and corresponding displays of hands-on material. When it comes to dealing with heavier equipment, the vulnerability of an extremity in a cast becomes a liability. The teacher is forced to rely on students. Obviously, teachers who are fortunate enough to have an assigned teacher's aide or a student teacher have an advantage. They can depend on the aide or an intern. The following is the story of a teacher who enlisted the help of two students.

> I was recovering from a broken arm. My right arm was still in a cast. Equipment was wheeled from place to place on one cart. Our school district could

not afford to have equipment in each classroom. I asked two students to be in charge of checking it out and bringing it to the room.

I picked out one student who was very annoying and known for disappearing during school. I also chose a student who was very responsible. I'm not sure why I chose them. I think they were sitting together. It worked out great. The student who was known for cutting school actually changed his behavior dramatically. I started using him in other situations as well. I don't know why he became more cooperative. I guess he felt needed. (Personal interview)

The Story of an Ice Cream Truck Selling BB Guns

KCRA News (2005) reports on a group of students working to make their school environment safer:

> Students at a Modesto school are banding together with a campaign to keep ice cream trucks from selling BB guns after one of their own was suspended for bringing a BB gun to school.
> The issue started when 11-year-old Santiago Sanchez brought a BB gun to Fairview Elementary School after purchasing it from an ice cream vendor. Sanchez was busted for bringing the gun to school.
> "Immediately, he was taken away from the classroom. Without further word, he was suspended for five days," said teacher Nick Keller.
> Sanchez said he wondered why it was so easy for children to buy toy guns from ice cream trucks. . . .
> So far, three students at Fairview Elementary School have been suspended in cases related to BB guns. And two students have been hit by BBs.
> Now, all of Santiago's fifth-grade class is rallying around him to try to ban the sale of toy guns to children. The students started "Project Citizen," putting together a petition and picket signs in preparation for a two-day protest against ice cream vendors . . . .
> Students plan to take the school's civic mission to the city council.

Santiago could be given a voice of importance protesting the manipulation of students from outside the schoolyard.

A Brief Story from the Life of Holly, Who Led Her Own Parent-Teacher Conference

Brodhagen (1995) shares a story about including her students:

> Everything was set. All student work portfolios were in order, the room was relatively pleasant, the table and chairs were in position, and I was nervous. "Will this really work?" I wondered. "Will these kids really conduct their own parent-student-teacher conferences? Had there really been enough preparation? Will parents want to listen to their child?"

> I glanced at the clock and knew it was time. My first conference was with Holly, a bright young adolescent who does consistently good work, but doesn't seem to want to participate in large- or small-group discussions.
>
> Holly walked into the room first and came right to the table and sat down. Trailing behind was her mother, who was carrying a younger sibling. I slid Holly's folder toward her, waiting for her to make introductions. "And who is this?" I asked, as I leaned over and touched the sibling's hand. With that, Holly began.
>
> Holly then read her written evaluation to her mom. When she had finished, she and her mom started to talk about why Holly didn't want to talk in front of her peers. Her mom admitted that, as a teenager, she didn't want to talk either. They talked about what was easy and challenging for Holly. They laughed about Holly's admission that doing her homework in front of the television wasn't such a good idea. And they discussed her goals for the next quarter, with Mom saying, "Holly tends to be too hard on herself."
>
> I just sat there, amazed. Holly said all I would have said, and much more that I never could or should. I simply validated a lot of what they said. When it was over, the three of us stood, smiling at one another, exchanging looks that seemed to say, "This felt good, let's do it again." (96–67)

Brodhagen was aware that conferences without the student present had not gone well when parents returned home to discuss what the teacher had told them. When the conference was negative, the student was usually grounded; if it went well, it was rarely discussed. "Together, we decided that conferences would focus on what students defined as their best work and also include a review of students' written evaluation and goals. . . . What really sets these conferences apart is that the students direct the action, from making necessary introductions and beginning the conference to wrapping up the discussion at the appropriate time" (p. 97).

Participants could be given a voice of importance by speaking before school board members, a curriculum committee, or a parent night about the construction of the parent-child conferences. Children are capable!

It is so easy, without fully realizing it, to only react to the negative behavior of children. A positive reaction to the child's good behavior will contribute to more desire on the child's part to continue cooperative behavior choices.

The learning curve includes much more than just academic knowledge to be reiterated on a chapter, semester, or standardized test. The development of courage, character, and positive protest cannot be measured; it can only be witnessed. Many parents and teachers are aware of this and use every creative means they have to make it known. Unfortunately, many remain unaware of the hidden potential of children.

Perhaps the most important quality that can be instilled in parents, teachers, and students is that of courage. Courage is needed to overcome obstacles that are important to democratic social living.

Each one of the children mentioned in this chapter reached deep into his or her heart and soul to contribute to the improvement of communities locally, nationally, and internationally. Viewing events through the eyes of a child is always a motivating experience. Children touch our hearts and souls in ways we never dreamed possible. The heart of our classrooms, families, and communities are the children that inhabit them.

When a school shooting takes place, the innocence of children is taken from them. Whether they are victims or witnesses to the horrific events, the entire school community, city, and state population is affected. News outlets from all over the nation report the tragedy, and listeners become subject to the aftermath of grief as well.

When a student is struggling, give the child a meaningful task. Step back and watch how the assignment comes together and how creative it is.

Chapter Four

Democratic Discussions with Children

"Democracy is not always convenient."—Deborah Meier

In many ways this chapter represents the practical aspects of what has been previously discussed: the devastation of school violence, the natural need for democratic expression on the part of adults as well as children, the historical precedent for a spirit of protest, an understanding of the postmodern culture we live in, and the capabilities of children throughout history as well as today. In this chapter, this information intersects with practicality.

Children are natural observers, becoming reliable conduits of information. They learn a great deal from experience, consuming knowledge in a short period of time. The school setting, available to all children from kindergarten through college, is a reliable, creative place for children to learn and practice democracy. Meier (1995) remarks that "all children could and should be inventors of their own theories, critics of other people's ideas, and makers of their own personal marks on this most complex world. It is an idea that is revolutionary. If we take it seriously" (p. 4).

Learning is foundational to young students. Teachers labor intensely to present curriculum that is easily understood and remembered. Unfortunately, many teachers are under continual pressure to teach material that will help pupils perform well on standardized testing. Effective teachers—which most aspire to be—are integral to our society. Educators realize that preparation for responsible citizenship is equally important as knowledge in a subject area. At some point, children will leave the tutelage of their teachers; hopefully, they will be equipped for responsible citizenship.

When children are allowed to voice their viewpoints in a welcoming environment, a lifelong interest in the democratic process is established. Democratic participation educates children in group decision making, teaches them to formulate opinions, and compels them to adapt to conclusions opposite to their own perspectives. The use of democratic principles in the classroom also increases and sustains cooperation.

Today's children want to be taken seriously. Unfortunately, in many families, classrooms, and community settings the opinions of children are overlooked. When children are given opportunities to form a viewpoint, disagree, discuss, and use consensus agreement, they make informed choices not only for themselves but also for their community. The model that children seek to follow is democracy.

Democracy reaches far deeper than just a political system; it can become an approach to everyday life. Democratic discussions can be a foundational strategy for giving children a voice of importance. Benson, Harkavy, and Puckett (2007), describing the beliefs of John Dewey, note that "Dewey theorized that only participatory democracy could produce the coerced, truly harmonious, organic society most conducive to both the common good and to individual self-development" (p. 4).

Teachers can enlist student participation in myriad ways: class meetings, opinions on methods of evaluation, realistic time frames for homework assignments, appropriate consequences for misbehavior, principles of self-encouragement as well as the encouragement of others, helping others in the greater community, and so on.

Creative ideas come to fruition as teachers and students set goals in an atmosphere of equality. The ultimate goal is to create learning experiences. Wolfgang and Glickman (1986) comment on democracy in the classroom: "[S]tudents need to practice democratic principles in school in order to learn how to contribute later to society as a whole. The central process modeling of democracy is the use of the class meeting. . . . Regular meetings should be held to discuss everyday occurrences as well as long-range policies" (p. 93).

In many ways, the school becomes a microcosm of society and how it maintains itself. In the words of Dewey (1964), "[T]he school itself shall be made a genuine form of active community life, instead of a place set apart in which to learn lessons".

EMPHASIS ON COMMUNITY

A focus of modernity was individualism and independence. Achievement was the volitional act of a single person in conjunction with predetermined goals. Postmodernity, on the other hand, places emphasis on the community in which individuals are participants in reaching mutual varying goals with the natural inclusion of diversity in its members. Fairholm (1998) views postmodern community as the "creation of harmony, making one out of many".

Metaphors centering on the words *school* and *community* have served as functional images dominating the creative thoughts of postmodern educators. Metaphors such as school as community, school as belonging, school as inclusion, school as safety, and school as spirituality have redefined schools. Cohen (1989) refers to the importance of metaphor stating that "[m]etaphors serve as powerful images that help shape culture, belief, and action" (p. 54).

SCHOOL AS COMMUNITY

In the past, modernistic schools existed regardless of the postmodern influence on society. A mistaken notion based on commonalities that existed between students—similar values, ethnicities, educational legacies, and, in some cases, general political positions—prevailed. The reality of most schools in the postmodern era is one of *difference* rather than *sameness*. Discussing the modernistic tendency toward a common center, Cohen (1989) writes, "It reflects the acceptance of a dominant center, a 'one best way' for articulating educational values and conducting educational practices to which all members of the school community should adhere" (p. 54).

Difference is primary to the metaphor for school as community. School as community promotes peaceful cooperation and advocates justice, interdependence, interconnection, belonging, and spaces of safety for growth and contribution. Furman (2002) describes community as "the ethics of acceptance of otherness with respect, justice and appreciation, and on peaceful cooperation within difference. It is inspired by the global community metaphor of an interconnected, interdependent web of people and cultures. It is fostered by processes that promote, among its members, belonging, trust of others and safety" (p. 83).

The following account, shared by a school counselor, is a practical example.

> A group of five students, headed for different universities, set a goal of scoring over 2000 on the SAT. They were comprised of three girls and two boys. Two of the students were Asian, one was African American, and the other two Caucasian. The parents were of different religious persuasions and cultural practices. The students enrolled in and finished preparatory classes together, spent hours of studying together and helped each other to stay energized and encouraged. All of them scored 2000 or better. (Personal interview)

The five students were more than a group; they were a learning community. They set a mutual goal even though the results would take them to different universities. Their cultural differences, with divergent religious expressions, customs, and viewpoints, were respected.

Preparatory classes, long hours of study, and a spirit of contribution to one another provided motivation as well as a sense of belonging and community. Rather than relying entirely on rugged individualism and independence, they accomplished their mutual goal using community effort. Spears (1998) writes about community effort, stating, "Community is about coming together in pursuit of some kind of purpose or some kind of goal that has meaning. . . . [S]ooner or later all of us are going to get to the point that 'I' can't survive unless 'we' choose we" (p. 250).

As previously stated, community also includes difference. The students cited in the aforementioned example were different in their religious backgrounds and countries of origin, but they were able to establish a mutual goal based on their common desire to achieve advanced scores on the SAT examinations. Respect for difference was demonstrated in their obvious diversity. The purely postmodern community, however, might also embrace students who possessed varying degrees of motivation.

The five students, when used only as a prime example, might run the risk of what Sergiovanni (1992) calls "centering." In other words, they were all driven students from similar economic backgrounds and were born to parents who viewed education as the single priority: "Communities are defined by their centers—repositories of values, sentiments, and beliefs that provide the needed cement for bonding people together in a cause" (p. 83).

It would be interesting to see what a similar group of students could contribute to an entire school district if they were given the opportunity to participate in discussing district guidelines to prepare for college admittance. In order to harness their experiences, however, they need to be given opportunities to present more than group testimonies of hard work. The chance to participate with school officials to create college preparatory materials would be an invaluable experience. Students with less motivation could also be included, giving perspective about the influences that create motivational deficits. Today's children are equipped to provide an important voice in solving relevant issues.

The digital age opens up the possibility of larger communities and consistent correspondence. Students interact during school hours and continue to text or post throughout the evening. Postmoderns are keenly adept at staying in touch with one another. This gives them an impressive influence on the same crucial issues that politicians, school officials, and community leaders are attempting to solve. It is entirely possible for a community of students to involve themselves digitally by using the internet as well as letters, petitions, and artistic posters. Postmoderns desire a voice on such issues as immigration, local pockets of poverty, and unfair school district policies that are open to public debate.

SCHOOL AS BELONGING

Belonging is an integral concept in creating community in the school as well as the classroom. The positive results of belonging have been studied by Dreikurs (1950) and Adler for decades. They were convinced that belonging was a primary desire of human nature. Belonging decreases the chances of perceived feelings of less-than because it provides the opportunity to receive and give encouragement. Adler and Dreikurs also suggested that misbehavior often stems from the lack of belonging in a social group.

According to Baumeister and Leary (1995), belonging impacts a multitude of positive attributes in students, including cognitive and emotional patterns, behavior, health, well-being, happiness, stress reduction, increase in helping relationships, positive attitude, respect toward others, acceptance of those who are not a part of their immediate friendship group, and a general perspective of kindness toward others. Those who do not experience acceptance are more likely to experience anxiety, depression, jealously, loneliness, higher rates of disadvantageous physical and mental health, and the negative consequences of drug and alcohol abuse. "The desire for interpersonal attachment may well be one of the most far-reaching and integrative constructs currently available to understand human nature" (p. 168).

Students who experience positive feelings of belonging can easily be motivated to make sure that every other child in the classroom is accepted. Perhaps a smaller group of students could form an acceptance team to befriend and show encouragement to those students who appear to be struggling.

Teachers can teach belonging and acceptance skills to the entire class and give students opportunities to activate these skills. When a teacher is aware of a child who is struggling, other children could be asked to reach out to the child using motives of genuine acceptance. According to Sergiovanni (1994), different types of community in schools may form: "They can become caring communities where members, motivated by altruistic love, make a total commitment to each other and where the characteristics that define their relationships are clearly gemeinschaft" (p. 5).

SCHOOL AS ENCOURAGEMENT

Alfred Adler and his esteemed colleague Rudolph Dreikurs did extensive work in the area of encouragement. Those who practice Adlerian psychology view encouragement as one of the most important therapeutic tools in family dynamics, the workplace, schools, and therapy. With regard to home and school, Dreikurs and Cassel (1972) write, "A child needs encouragement like a plant needs sun and water. Unfortunately, those who need encouragement the most get it the least because they behave in such a way that our reaction to them pushes them further into discouragement and rebellion" (p. 49).

Encouragement is action oriented, even though the foundation is existence based. The child needs only to be present to experience encouragement when teachers begin "catching"—intentionally looking for—positive behaviors that the child demonstrates. Even before the process begins, an encouraging parent or teacher fundamentally believes that each child possesses positive attributes that can contribute to the greater good of all students.

A misbehaving child is a discouraged child. Oftentimes a discouraged child interprets negative responses by others as signs of personal criticism. Many of these children internalize negative responses with the self-talk statement, "Since you see me in a negative way, I might as well act in a negative way." Discouraged children mistakenly live up to negative labels creating an antagonistic place of belonging. According to Dreikurs and Cassel (1972), "The essence of encouragement is to increase the child's confidence in himself and to convey to him that he is good enough as he is, not just as he might be" (p. 49).

The following methods of encouragement are helpful:

* Greet each child warmly.
* Look for genuine effort and make a comment emphasizing improvement.
* Look for and point out effort, not just results.
* Ask the child to help you with something important.
* Show trust in the child.
* Communicate that everyone makes mistakes.

"Success breeds fulfillment, self-acceptance, and the belief that one can achieve. Frustration and discouragement lead to suppressed aggression or to aggressive action, conflict and defiant behavior" (Dreikurs and Cassel, p. 59).

SCHOOL AS SPIRITUALITY

In the postmodern era, religion is recognized as a powerful force in the lives of parents, students, and teachers. Generally speaking, in the modernistic era, religion was only defined as commitment to a deity or deities and might also contain historical narratives. Spirituality, a postmodern descriptive word, on the other hand, includes sensitivity, connection, association, and attraction to something greater.

Connection is extremely important in the quest for postmodern spirituality—connection with people, nature, the universe, or God. Many postmoderns desire an experience with religion rather than didactic explanations of it.

SCHOOL AS PARTICIPATION

When children arrive at school, they are immediately thrust into a group of fellow students. Myriad associations appear. A typical day is composed of individual and group assignments. Students learn that cooperation is essential. Fellow students are opinionated as well as competitive. Most teachers are aware of the challenge in guiding classroom participants into topic-oriented discussions.

Participation in group settings allows space for learning as well as discussions that contribute to the classroom atmosphere. The classroom is a microcosm that gives helpful insights into the world that exists outside the classroom and the school.

Democratic Discussions in the Elementary Classroom

The elementary school classroom offers a productive setting for children to gain firsthand experience in the democratic process. Class meetings provide a venue for experiencing democratic practices in the classroom. Many schools operate from a homeroom format where students congregate in the same classroom to begin each day. During this time, plans for the day are often discussed and most students are eager for the day to unfold. Hopefully, the children are well-rested and adequately nourished.

If possible, it is helpful to conduct the class meeting at the same time each week. Eventually, students will look forward to it because it provides a forum where they can actively communicate observations, ideas, and possible solutions. Dinkmeyer, McKay, and Dinkmeyer Jr. (1980) communicate three reasons for establishing class meetings: planning, problem solving, and encouragement. Class meetings emulate democratic group meetings: Everyone functions as an equal at such meetings, and participants encourage and help each other.

Problem solving is instructional for life. Many disciplinary situations at home and school are enforced with dictatorial mandates. Some hold the view that democracy is fine for government and society, but not meant for home or school.

Teachers who show the courage to allow the students to share in the decision-making process create many advantages. First, when a misbehaving child (usually a child who lacks a feeling of belonging) participates in a class meeting, he or she develops a feeling of belonging. Second, the misbehavior (which is likely bothering most of the students) is being addressed. And third, other students become more tolerant and positive toward discouraged children. Dreikurs, Grunwald, and Pepper (1982) share the following democratic discussion in a Montessori school classroom.

"Candy was missing from the shelf. It would normally be distributed to the class each day. Desiring to solve the issue in a democratic fashion, the teacher asked the class for help. It was addressed as a general problem so names were not mentioned. The input from the children was free-flowing, and the atmosphere was welcoming."

One student suggested the child sit in the corner. However, the teacher kindly mentioned that the corner had nothing to do with the actual candy. Another child believed that telling his mother would be a way to handle it. Once again, the teacher simply stated that the boy's mother didn't really have anything to do with the candy that was taken. Giving the children a hint, the teacher encouraged the class to focus directly on the behavior. "After more punitive suggestions, one child came up with the idea of leaving this child out in the receiving of candy on the day he already had his share. This was discussed with the entire group until they all came to a consensus" (p. 126).

Nelsen, Lott, and Glenn (1997) share another example of a democratic discussion. In this particular situation, the student was asked to leave the room because the teacher was fearful that fellow classmates might be overly critical. The discussion began with a question: "What kind of problems are you having with Stephen?"

After the students shared many answers, a second question was asked: "Do you have any idea why Stephen might do these things?" The answers were insightful, ranging from acting like a bully to acting with mean behavior. One child even posed the answer that it was because he was a foster child.

The teacher then asked, "Do you have any idea what it might feel like to be a foster child?" This question motivated the children to think about Stephen's living situation; he was with a new family, living in a completely different part of the city.

One of the final questions motivated the children into action. "How many of you would be willing to help Stephen?" Every hand went up as students shared friendly ideas to encourage him. Needless to say, his behavior became much more positive. When asked, the children shared perceptive ideas that were the equal to ideas adults would have. "They are able to accomplish more than any one teacher, foster parent, principal, or counselor. The kids are powerful in what they can do to help" (p. 153).

Learning mutual respect is one of the primary goals of class meetings. The teacher gives direction, helps each student to participate confidently, and is responsible for guiding the class as a whole to follow up on agreements. The teacher models kindness and firmness while making sure students avoid fighting or yielding on group consensus decisions. Acceptance of others and oneself is also an important goal. Working for human dignity and mutual respect as well as helping one another are direct results of this goal. Shared responsibility is another outcome. Unfortunately, teachers sometimes end up either autocratically forcing their will or allowing children to prevail over them.

Glasser (1986) notes that decisions about curriculum and rules should include input from children. Living out principles of democracy is extremely important. It places responsibility on children to contribute to a better school by solving problems together. Glasser believed that children feel a responsibility to find solutions to the issues they face.

Democratic Discussions in a College Class Community

A few years ago, I was teaching as an adjunct at a major university. It was important to teach the students firsthand what democracy could mean in a college classroom as well as in the classrooms they would soon inhabit as new teachers. The class needed to decide methods of evaluation, test score categories, and attendance requirements. It was prudent to deal with these three areas in order to follow university standards. The democratic process enthusiastically commenced.

The students who loved the challenge of memory recall led the cause. They suggested two objective tests (true/false and multiple choice). Those students who loved the challenge of writing about the why or why not of an issue countered with the suggestion of an essay test and a term paper. Essentially it was a contest between factually oriented learners and conceptually oriented learners. Educational research has proven that both are valid styles of learning according to the numerous personality type and learning style studies that have been conducted by reputable colleges and universities over the years.

Before the process began, the class agreed on a consensus style of democratic process, since a direct vote would leave out those students who were still mired in the drop/add process. The participation of the students was overwhelming and exhaustive as they worked through the process in an orderly and respectful fashion. It was obvious that very few of the students had ever participated in this kind of forum. The students—maybe for the first time—believed that their opinions were valuable and helpful.

The students also began to understand and accept the learning styles of their fellow classmates. Before the discussion concluded, students with opposite approaches to learning were actually supporting each other. Through respectful dialogue, they were able to see the question from other students' point of view.

The student-led results were as follows: One objective test (for those who relished the accumulation of facts), one essay test (for those who like to purport and defend ideas), a team project (for those students who have a propensity for creativity); test score results (revealed only in numbers) would be written on the blackboard and the students (before knowing their individual scores) would by consensus decide the breakdown of As, Bs, Cs, and so on.

It was interesting to see how many other instructors from whom this particular group of students had taken classes also employed a consensus-type democracy in constructing class procedures. According to a show of hands, very few of them had ever encountered this process. In other class settings, class policies and procedures appeared to be decided upon by the instructor rather than by student consensus. During the first session of classes with other instructors, according to the students, a syllabus was distributed that described the course and the method by which students would be evaluated. There was rarely a democratic discussion of any substance. It is doubtful that the instructors had any premeditated intention to teach as the sole authority who determined every aspect of the class; nonetheless, their courses were bereft of any democratic participation.

An irrational fear on the part of instructors (or teachers at any grade level) might be that the students would come to a consensus to do very little. Inherent in the democratic process, however, is the idea of freedom within limits. Most students in the class participated responsibly in the creation of realistic guidelines. The simple fact that their ideas were respected, given serious consideration, and then activated created more motivation. Students can solve most issues that confront them in a school setting.

Discussions about Community Concerns

Many communities, whether inner city, suburban, or rural, have concerns about the people living in them. Long lists of needed improvements are compiled. Children have a creative opportunity to shed light on the development of ideas.

- *The school setting:* Rules for library use; creating popular programs for libraries such as drama, puppetry, tutoring young children, library tours, etc.; when to start and end the school year; healthy menus for school lunches; additional after-school programs; ideas for back-to-school nights; involvement in school board meetings; inclusion programs for students with different countries of origin; and more parent involvement.
- *The medical community:* Programs for child cancer victims and survivors, volunteerism in children's hospitals, senior citizen safety, and vaccination awareness.
- *The community at large*: Involvement in historical societies and sites, landscaping in public areas, town hall meetings, space for authoring articles in local newspapers and magazines, and greater cooperation in the classroom and school.

These lists can certainly be expanded. Dreikurs and Cassel (1972) state, "We can teach responsibility only by giving the pupils opportunities to accept responsibilities themselves" (p. 78).

Democratic Discussions in the Family

One of three types of parenting styles generally develops as new parents begin their journey in raising children: autocratic, laissez-faire, or democratic. Autocratic parenting provides little opportunity for children to participate. Most decisions are made by the parents, or in some cases, by only one parent. There are major drawbacks to this parenting style. In a subtle way, the autocratic parent shows disrespect for children. The pernicious message is: "Since you are incapable of making mature decisions, I will make them for you."

This top-down method leaves others completely out of the process. However, learning to state one's opinion, making a stand in support of the opinion, and hearing the point of view of others teaches children that contrary opinions have validity. When a decision is made through consensus, the child learns to adapt to another alternative.

Children raised in an autocratic home are more dependent on outside influences for structure and often struggle in making everyday decisions. They become dependent on being told what to do. Dinkmeyer and Dreikurs (1963) note, "Our method of dealing with children . . . is based on tradition. Our tradition was autocratic. Every deficiency, every failure, traditionally considered a violation of demands and obligations not to be tolerated by the authorities who established them. . . . As a consequence of the tradition, we all know well how to find fault, to degrade, to retaliate, to humiliate and exhort. But when it comes to encouragement, we are inept and unqualified" (pp. 117–18).

Some children raised in these homes react against dictatorial practices in the home by adopting the completely opposite approach of laissez-faire parenting as adults themselves. In this parenting style, freedom within limits is a concept that is rarely discussed; consequently, unabated freedom exists and mutual respect is rarely experienced.

Laissez-faire parenting gives parents very little influence over the guidelines and consequences of misbehavior. Mutual agreements are nonexistent. Conversations with children about cooperative behavior toward others and respect for rules are not prioritized.

Gottman (1997) summarizes, "Children do not learn to regulate their emotions. They can have trouble concentrating, forming (or keeping) friendships, getting along with other children and respecting others. The pressure to parent according to others' desires can lead to an inauthentic connection and a laissez-faire approach to parenting" (p. 43).

Laissez-faire parenting influences children to think only of themselves. Often, they are rescued by parents rather than experiencing a natural or logical consequences. They see no use for mutual agreements since they are not interested in following them. They know their parents are unlikely to follow through on them as well. This approach lacks the structure that is needed for healthy maturity.

Unquestionably, the most effective parenting approach is a democratic one. Not only does it work, but it also emulates what children learn in textbooks, view on television, and hear parents and teachers discussing. Democracy is at the heart of the American personality. Unfortunately, many parents and teachers are fearful of losing control of students at home or in the classroom. The concern, however, is usually exaggerated. Mayhem rarely results when children are allowed to use democratic principles to solve matters of family events, rules, and consequences.

The beginning point for adults is accepting the child both physically and emotionally. When a four-year-old (or younger) toddles off to school, an approach to life and a host of opinions are developing, and early knowledge about power and authority is being experienced. The phrase "out of the womb into the world" is full of sights, sounds, observations, and new associations.

The greatest challenge for very young children is that they are small in stature and must begin a mistake-filled pilgrimage to find a place of belonging. Children quickly observe adults as taller, stronger, more intelligent, and even having a language that others respond to. Young children, consequently, develop perceived feelings of less-than and then spent most of their lives compensating for those feelings. As Adler (1998) notes, "At the very basis of a child's development lies his struggle to compensate for his weakness; a thousand talents and capabilities arise from our feelings of inadequacy" (p. 28).

In metaphorical language, respect for the capabilities of children has innumerable tentacles. Children observe, interpret, categorize, and contribute opinions and ideas as strategies to overcome their keen awareness that they live in a world where most people are more skillful than they are. Since all children are striving to find a place to fit in, they have an insatiable desire to contribute.

When children are given a chance to equally contribute, they discover a place of belonging, significance, and respect. It is likely these children will contribute responsibly as adults. The family and the classroom provide practical spaces for democratic living. Dinkmeyer and McKay (1973) provide helpful concepts with regard to the value of family meetings such as family events, planning and decision making, problems that are repeated, working together on household needs, expressing feelings about change, encouragement, and sharing experiences in social living.

Emphasis on community, belonging, encouragement, spirituality, and participation are essential to staying encouraged and encouraging others. Encouraging others is contagious. Devoting a day at school, at home, or in the workplace to emphasizing principles of encouragement will reveal the positive aspects of it.

Chapter Five

Bullying

The Exaggerated Need for Power and Control

"The laws of human society are a closed book to children inadequately equipped to take their place in it. They have a keen sense of life's hostility which they unconsciously exaggerate . . . they demand an extraordinary amount of attention and of course they think far more of themselves than others." —Alfred Adler

Bullying other children represents a lack of positive contribution within the family or school community. Aggression toward others is not something that is natural to children; instead, it is a tendency they develop. Children have a natural desire to belong and strive toward feelings of significance and contribution. Unfortunately, these feelings sometimes lack mature development. That is to say, children, due to factors contributing to discouragement, are unable to develop healthy ways to contribute to others. Adler (1956) states, "We have always to reckon with others, to adapt ourselves to others, and to interest ourselves in them" (p. 13).

BRIEF HISTORY OF ADLERIAN PSYCHOLOGY

Many theorists provide explanations about violent behavior in schools. However, the work of Alfred Adler and his colleague Rudolf Dreikurs provides the most comprehensive information regarding this topic. Adler discusses the following influences: the role of the family model, inferiority (feelings of less-than), lifestyle development, birth order, belonging, and social interest. It is important to note, however, as stated by Mosak and Maniacci (1999), that "Adlerian psychology, advocates a soft determinism; one can only speak of probabilities, not certainties" (p. 38).

It was Adler's belief that behavior is not caused; however, influences on choices of behavior are real. Likewise, school shootings are not directly caused, but the shooters have been negatively influenced by life experiences. Adler believed that people attach individual meaning to experiences. In other words, it is not the literal experience that causes behavior choices; rather, it is the meaning the individual attaches to the experience. The following account regarding Adler's life gives perspective about the role of experiential influences, illustrating the meaning Adler attached to his own life experiences. Mosak, H. & Maniacci, M. (1999) offer the following biography.

Adler attaches meaning to his life experiences.

Alfred Adler was born on February 7, 1870, in Vienna. His father was a Jewish grain merchant. He was the third child and the second boy born to the family. His childhood experiences included the death of a younger brother in a room they shared, rivalry with his firstborn brother, and dealing with the illnesses of rickets, pneumonia, and poor eyesight.

Medical challenges prompted him to become a doctor. He became an ophthalmologist (as a result of his own poor eyesight), transitioned into general practice (to gain insights into his own near-death experience from pneumonia), and eventually became interested in psychiatry. Adler's clients included circus people, who influenced his perspectives on individuals' capacity to compensate for unusual physical strengths and weaknesses.

The historically documented Wednesday Night Meetings began in 1902 with three members: Adler, Carl Jung, and Sigmund Freud. The group eventually became the Viennese Psychoanalytic Society. Adler opposed Freud's psychoanalytic theory and his demand for unwavering allegiance to it. After his departure, Adler founded the Society for Individual Psychology, which holds the premise that each individual is a whole being.

As a medical field officer in World War I, Adler witnessed firsthand the ravages of war. One of the foundational concepts of individual psychology, social interest, resulted from this experience. After the war, he was instrumental in creating child guidance clinics in the Vienna Public Schools to educate teachers, counselors, social workers, and physicians in educational reform and therapeutic education.

In 1932 Adler acquired a teaching position in medical psychology at Long Island College of Medicine. He moved his family to the United States in 1934. In 1937, at the age of sixty-seven, Adler died of a heart attack while on a lecture tour in Aberdeen, Scotland.

HELPFUL TERMS IN ADLERIAN PSYCHOLOGY

Social context refers to the concept that a person cannot be adequately evaluated from his or her social situation. Individuals are socially embedded. Behavior is never isolated from the social situation in which it occurs.

Goal directed behavior is the purposeful direction of behavior. All behavior moves in the direction of conscious and misunderstood goals created by the individual. Adler believed that we are not driven by the past but are pulled by future goals and purposes.

Lifestyle is an approach to life that originates in earliest childhood. Adler believed that during the experiences of childhood, a unique approach to life is established that determines how one responds within the environment. Lifestyle is the overall psychological movement toward one's goals. Negative experiences from childhood can alter the perceptions of the original lifestyle belief.

The style of life has a great deal to do with the perspective we create to find our places to fit into the world we live. The perspectives a child creates may not be objectively true. As Dreikurs (1972) states, however, "All opinions are correct from the point of view of the observer" (p. 21). Mosak and Maniacci (1999) suggest three core functions of the life-style: to help us understand life, "it gives us a chance to predict life, and it provides us with the opportunity to control life" (p. 168).

The following statements are possible indicators of a child's approach to life: "I must control"; "I am superior"; "I am entitled"; "I don't count"; "I must be perfect." The mistaken logic of these statements is based on false conclusions about the desire to belong. For instance, children who believe they must attain power to control others live with the mistaken notion that power will provide a place of significance, albeit a negative place.

Children who must control are likely to show aggression toward other children. Hostility becomes a strategy to gain the power to control. An example of the child's self-talk might be, "I feel most important and valuable when I show power to win or control."

Social interest involves the positive movement of behavior in the direction of others. Adler believed that the condition of an individual's mental health is connected to the degree of social interest that has been developed. Social interest (community feeling) is the cornerstone of Adlerian theory.

Private logic refers to the interpretation of events that affect the person. Individualized evaluation of self, others, and the world are activated.

The individual might not be fully aware of her or his purpose in displaying the behavior until it is pointed out.

Feelings of inferiority (perceived feelings of less-than) are universal to all; however, when an individual becomes overwhelmed by these feelings, useful participation in society is hindered. When the individual compensates in positive ways, feelings of inferiority can propel the person forward. On the other hand, when the individual overcompensates, using superiority to deal with the feelings, self-esteem can be affected negatively.

Tasks of life represent challenges in life. Adler categorized three life tasks: work (a useful occupation), friendship (meaningful involvement with others), and love (realizing one's role in marriage and family). Overcoming routine obstacles in life is important to this principle as well.

Early recollections (first memories) represent something important to the individual. They have a bearing on the individual's life as he or she views it. Early memories communicate an individual's basic view of life. They can provide information about early perceptions of lifestyle (approach to life) development.

FAMILY MODEL

Parents often raise children in the same way they were parented. The lack of discernible empathy in an abused child's family has a direct impact on the child's self-concept. The child who finds it impossible to find favor in the eyes of a parent will likely develop an increased sense of inferiority. Perceived feelings of less-than eventually impact hostile movement toward other children. A false notion about using power negatively helps a child cope in a family where aggression toward others is normal.

The intergenerational acts of aggression within a family can usually be traced back to the parents and often to the grandparents, who also experienced abuse. Parents who were abused mistakenly internalize the notion that aggression works, salving personal frustration and forcing children into compliance.

Physical altercations followed by expressions of hugs and kisses (generally at a later time) teach children that abuse is an expression of love and acceptance. Usually, parents who raise their children in this fashion were unable to get their own emotional needs met in a positive way. Since they were abused as children, they likely perceive the world in hostile ways.

The abuse heaped on their own children can become a necessary strategy for dealing with their own feelings of inferiority. Hitchcock (1987) provides a helpful summary about the generational cycle of abuse: "Abuse is seen as normal and can lead to developmental deficits and inadequate coping skills" (p. 54). Abuse can be a significant influence on a child's basic approach to life.

Regardless of the community, the desire for acknowledgment is almost innate. Two options exist: behavior that contributes to others in a useful way or behavior that contributes to others in a useless way.

FAMILY CONSTELLATION

It was Adler's belief that a child's position in the family constellation has the most impact on the child's lifestyle or approach to life (Ansbacher & Ansbacher, 1956).

The First Child

Oldest children are born into families without older sibling models to emulate. Consequently, they are left to interpret the responses of the adults who surround them without the collaboration of other family members. They like to please—often imitating the behavior important to their parents. Sometimes parents unknowingly put pressure on oldest children to become high achievers; children mistakenly view this as perfectionism. Firstborn children are also skilled with details and like to set goals. They are often opinionated and like to express their viewpoints. Generally, they live life with a serious mindset.

The firstborn child is the only child in a family to go through psychological dethronement. When a second child is born, the family atmosphere drastically changes. The firstborn child no longer has the undivided attention of the parents as the new infant's needs take precedence. The new infant is often viewed as a threat, and the oldest child becomes preoccupied with developing strategies to remind the new sibling that "first is first." A change in territorial position is not an option in the mind of a firstborn.

Adler (1931) was one of the first practitioners to research birth order, writing, "Sometimes a child who has lost his power, the small kingdom he ruled, understands better than others the importance of power and authority. . . . [P]ower should always be preserved in the hands of those entitled to it" (p. 151). A dethroned, angry firstborn is a likely candidate for bullying others.

The Second Child

The second child is born into a situation quite different than the first. This child has to share the parents' attention with another child who has already taken up residency. The second child, who has no frame of reference for having the undivided attention of the parents, develops acceptance of the other child. A hidden motive, however, is to spend life trying to overtake the firstborn. The oldest child, on the other hand, views the firstborn position as irreversible, regardless of any strategies the second child creates.

The second child is often easy to recognize. This child appears to be in a perpetual state of running, racing, and competing to catch up with the oldest. The second child feels slighted and is energized by self-talk that states: "I'll show you"; "We will see about that"; or "This is a long way from being over." The second child believes that overthrowing the firstborn is always a possibility.

Second-born children are often crafty in their strategies to overtake the first child. One of many tactics is to consistently praise the older sibling. This sets a standard that is difficult for the oldest child to reach and maintain. Parents become disappointed with the oldest child and verbal altercations can occur. As a skilled observer of mistakes, the second-born will do the opposite of the oldest child's mistakes and then verbally acknowledge his or her own praiseworthy behavior.

The arrival of a third child into the family creates a new set of complications for the second child. The second-born is launched into the squeezed child position and must live between two siblings who have natural importance simply because of their positions in the family. When the third child is the firstborn boy or the firstborn girl in the family, parents are jubilant: "We are elated; we now have our first boy!" or "We finally have a girl for Mom!"

The new situation has both positives and negatives. On the positive side, the second-born will learn the skills of reconciliation by living between an older child and a younger child. This child learns the skill of compromise, which is helpful when moving through life. On the negative side, the second-born has to always strive to keep up with the first child while staying ahead of the third one.

Squeezed children, who are unable to find a positive place of belonging, can easily become discouraged. They often mistakenly find a negative place of belonging, displaying misbehavior to attain the label of difficult child. Showing aggression toward other children in the form of verbal or physical actions provides a sense of significance. When this child is given the label of bully, it can become woven into the child's lifestyle.

The Youngest Child

The last-born is the only child who will never have to go through psychological dethronement by the birth of another child. The last-born child will always remain the baby of the family, given an inordinate amount of attention simply because he or she was the last one to arrive.

The baby of the family can be a formidable force to be reckoned with by other siblings. Youngest children are often seen as cute and have very few difficulties living up to the label. More often than not, last-born children have fewer expectations placed on them. It is not uncommon for a youngest child to have a newer car earlier than other siblings, fewer household requirements with very little accountability, and a nonexistent curfew.

In birth order theory, youngest children usually have three distinct character qualities: they are often charismatic, perceptive, and manipulative. Last-born children are also skillful at enticing others to take care of them. Often they create their own unique approaches to life: "I might be the last, but I refuse to be the least." They track the victories and defeats of other siblings for future use, when they can use the information to overcome older siblings.

Youngest children could be prone to bullying. Indulgence is usually the guilty culprit. The parents and all other siblings contribute significantly to the indulgence. Spoiled children, who rarely have a chance to become independent, often lack the confidence and courage to accomplish tasks on their own. Lack of confidence reins supreme. They might set goals and desire specific accomplishments, but the degree to which they are expected to reach the goals an accomplishments is not as defined as it sometimes is with other birth order positions. Sometimes, unlike other siblings, they are not allowed to experience logical and natural consequences.

The last-born child, therefore, might become the family manipulator—or at school, the classroom bully. According to Adler (1931), "The second largest proportion of problem children comes from the youngest" (p. 379).

Only Children

Only children are sometimes the most challenging to deal with. They do not have to share with siblings. They become frustrated when parents are not available to meet an immediate need. Only children have their parents' undivided attention and travel most places with them. The concept of a babysitter is often somewhat foreign to them. Only children live under very high expectations. They are treated as little adults and are expected to act accordingly.

Only children might be expected to achieve at perfectionist levels. When they are unable to achieve this lofty goal, they might resort to lesser goals and become involved in activities that require much less effort. Aggressiveness toward other children could become one such behavior, especially when the desire to please fails or the effort to please is ignored.

Twins

Twins will always hold a special place in family and educational settings. When they are identical twins, the "specialness" factor is even greater. Identical twins sometimes can have difficulty developing separate identities; they are often referred to simply as "the twins." Identical twins are held in high esteem and usually receive unsolicited attention. Unless a fierce competition exists between them, with an obvious loser or winner, twins are not usually combative toward others. A silent accountability between the two of them is helpful in preventing misbehavior.

The Pampered Child

While the pampered child is not a birth order position, these children none-theless develop strategies that will help them achieve success. Very often, to the pampered child other people become a means to an end in attaining a superior position over others. In this way, the child becomes dependent on others to achieve success.

Adler mentions potential negatives developed by the pampered child: extreme discouragement, continuous hesitation, oversensitivity, impatience, exaggerated emotion, and physical and psychological disturbances showing the signs of weakness and need for support.

Due to the pampered child's dependence on others for achievement, this child does not want to lose relationships with peers. The pampered child has obstacles in life to conquer. However, these children are not likely to become classroom bullies because other children are necessary resources for the achievement of goals.

Dreikurs and Stoltz (1964) make the point that "the interpretation a child makes about his position within the family . . . can be as infinite as human creativity permits" (p. 34). Each child individually interprets the events of life, regardless of his or her birth order position.

SOCIAL INTEREST

Social interest is the cornerstone of Adlerian psychology. Adler (1956) intro-duced this concept in the word *Gemeinschaftsgeful*, which is translated as "community feeling." Lundin (1989) explains this concept as social feeling, communal feeling, communal intention, community interest, and social inter-est. The following is a list of examples.

- Moving toward others with kindness and communicating encouragement to others.
- Demonstrating a genuine commitment to friendship, romantic relation-ships, and cooperation in the work setting.
- Showing empathy for people in difficult situations, lamenting about world hunger and peace, showing grief for the death of a loved one, a working

commitment to environmental issues, the desire to leave the world in a better place, and actions of helpful participation in group or individual situations.

Conversely, when students or adults show a lack of cooperation, social interest is lacking. Social interest is somewhat natural to most children and adults; however, it does require nurture and encouragement.

Aggression or hostility, as a pattern of behavior, measures the degree of social interest that is yet to be developed. When individuals think only of themselves, social interest is nonexistent. Students who consistently bully other students show an obvious deficit in social interest.

Children and adults alike live in a social context where constant cooperation is needed. The child's ability to live in accordance with others depends a great deal on how the child views other people: as a threat or as an asset. Children who bully other children see others as threats. Children who are aggressive toward others are often camouflaging a great deal of inferiority and discouragement.

DISCOURAGEMENT AND ITS NEGATIVE CONSEQUENCES

Sadly, school shootings and other violent behavior are occurring more frequently. The one diagnosis that can be made is that the perpetrator is deeply discouraged. More often than not, the person is disheartened, lacking any form of recognition. The individual mistakenly perceives that the only way to become noticed—to feel significant and important—is to act out with violent behavior.

A common misconception is that students who are severely dispirited are also significantly depressed and might be on a suicidal path. In most cases, an opposite action is foremost in the individual's thoughts: The premeditated behavior is to show power and superiority, and a gun, knife, or other powerful weapon becomes part of the plan.

People who choose to display violent behavior have been unable to develop social interest. At every turn, they mistakenly perceive rejection and defeat. Myriad reasons for this exist: perceived feelings of less-than, physical or emotional abuse in the family, exaggerated hatred, social prejudice, and so on.

Often children, high school students, or adults perceive a tangible paralysis in their ability to create any meaningful social movement. Social acceptance seems unattainable. More often than not, however, this is not the case. It is usually not the social encounter itself that is a determining factor; rather, it is the individual's interpretation of the incident that makes a difference.

Any individual, regardless of age, who perceives continual intimidation and criticism will inevitably strive to fight back.

Dreikurs & Cassel (1972) write about the four goals of misbehavior. Attention getting is based on the child's subjective interpretation that becoming the center of attention provides status. The child's faulty logic is that status is only attainable by exhibiting attention-getting behavior.

The second mistaken goal of misbehavior is power struggle. This occurs when the child's demand for undue attention falls short. The faulty logic self-talk states, "If you don't let me do what I want, I must not be important." Temper tantrums, unnecessary arguments, and refusal to cooperate are just a few of the behavior choices that are prevalent.

The third goal of mistaken behavior is revenge. The revenge seeking child desires to hurt others as a way of feeling important. The behavior can be violent, vicious and destructive. The child might injure others as a method of establishing importance.

The fourth goal of ill-conceived behavior is simply to give up attempting to achieve productive behavior. The child is convinced that she or he can do nothing that is ever good enough. Consequently, the child simply quits trying. Failed attempts at success is the result.

Revenge, the third goal of misbehavior, is the only mistaken goal that requires premeditation. The mistaken goal of the behavior is to show power and superiority by harming others. This is generally the category that school shooters will emerge (p. 34–39).

CREATING AN IMPERFECT COMMUNITY

Perfectionism stalks us all. As discussed earlier, our first exposure to the land of giants contributes to our perceived feelings of less-than. Also discussed was our need to find a place of belonging. These two concepts work in partnership with one another. In order to find a place of belonging, the child must compensate for being small, unskilled, and inadequate. The danger is when the child overcompensates and perfectionism enters the picture.

The child then sets unrealistic standards, attaching self-worth to the accomplishment of unattainable goals. These perfectionist achievement standards are impossible to reach, leaving the child overwhelmingly discouraged. Often, the child develops self-talk that says, "Since I can't be perfect, it makes no sense to even try." The child becomes envious of those who do succeed, usually developing a critical approach to them. Bullying can become manifest in verbally criticizing others. When bullying becomes physical, the individual has become even more discouraged.

When an atmosphere of imperfection is developed, the child will no longer attempt to be perfect. Dreikurs & Cassel (1972) note, "Undefeatable courage is the courage to be imperfect" (p. 49). It is important to note that accepting imperfection is not a substitute for hard work and genuine effort.

Imperfection is everywhere. As children and adults accept imperfection in themselves, they are more likely to accept imperfection in others. Acknowledgment of imperfection develops a spirit of equal respect.

Eliminating the need to set unreachable standards also eliminates a great deal of discouragement. Children and adults can realistically evaluate themselves and learn from mistakes. Accepting imperfection helps children and high school students avoid needlessly criticizing others. Sometimes, students who bully are discouraged perfectionists who are taking the anger they feel for themselves out on others: "If I can't be perfect in my accomplishments, maybe I can be the perfect bully."

Problem children often create behavior issues that affect the entire classroom. Essentially, children and high school students who show patterns of misbehavior are discouraged in how they perceive others seeing them and how they see themselves in relationship to others. Often this discouragement is the result of the person's inability to meet perfectionist achievements that are self-imposed or set by adults.

The commonality of imperfection enhances group discussion as well. Some perspectives might be more helpful than others. In a group of imperfect viewpoints, each opinion is welcomed. It is empowering for students to know their thoughts will be welcomed.

Similar to adult discussions, differences will occur. When students realize that both differences and agreements have some degree of imperfection in them, the atmosphere becomes less competitive. Children realize that a co-equal, respectful discussion has nothing to do with grade point average, class popularity, or the number of friends one has. Imperfection is experienced by all. With regard to teachers, who are the leaders in any classroom setting, Dreikurs, Grunwald, & Pepper (1982) state, "A teacher cannot be a good leader unless she has the inner freedom and unless she can admit that she herself has made a mistake" (p. 145).

Creating a community of imperfection will not completely eliminate bullying behaviors, but it will reduce the need individuals feel to control and win. It will also diminish mistaken perspectives about the desire to feel superior, perceived feelings of less-than, and the exaggerated need for power.

THE CRUCIAL ROLE OF ENCOURAGEMENT

One of the foundational concepts of Adler and Dreikurs is the role of encouragement given to children by adults, parents, and teachers. Encouragement is vital because of children's perceived need for perfectionism, which leads to a feeling of defeat because perfection is unattainable.

Striving for perfection is common to everyone. Life demands that we develop the skills and abilities necessary to perform daily tasks competently. Overcoming perceived feelings of less-than has two distinct components: first, to compensate for physical limitations, and second, to overcome perceived psychological inadequacies.

Striving becomes the vehicle of action. Living in the land of giants requires that children master walking, talking, eating, dressing, and navigating daily obstacles. In the psychological realm, the quest is seeking to be a part of the social living functions that are already in motion. Individuals are confronted with diverse and complicated tasks: communicating, working, learning, laughing, agreeing, disagreeing, and cooperatiing with perceived social criteria for acceptance.

The dilemma is how to accomplish this goal, and the trap we fall into is the perception that it must be done perfectly. What stalks us relentlessly is striving tirelessly to change the −1 of obvious weakness to the +1 of faultless strength. The mistaken notion is that we must overcome the obstacles of life perfectly. The accomplishment of an individual's greatest assets can become nagging weaknesses when they are perceived as imperfect.

Adler (1931) states, "This feeling, this longing for the abrogation of every imperfection, is never absent" (p. 103). And so we strive with tireless effort to move from a position of inferiority to superiority. This journey begins from the earliest point of infancy.

THE PROCESS OF ENCOURAGEMENT

Children who misbehave are essentially discouraged. They often feel a lack of attention and significance. Their choices of behavior reflect the mistaken idea that negative attention is better than very little attention. Misbehavior can be changed to positive behavior when parents or teachers develop the skills of encouragement.

- Point out strengths, not weaknesses: "You are working hard at turning in your assignments on time." This places the emphasis on the action, not the result. Students are well aware of the errors they make. Their mistaken choices have been the topic of numerous discussions about them. But students are often unaware of the strengths they show because they are swallowed up in the negativity of the moment. Parents and teachers can lose sight of cooperative efforts on the part of the individual as well, creating a detrimental cycle of discouragement.
- Catch the student making a positive contribution and briefly make a comment on it: "I appreciate your perspective in our group discussions." Priority is placed on the word *catch*. Essentially, it means the parent, teacher, or

fellow student is actively looking for the positives in the individual. Pointing out positive actions and attributes in others becomes a philosophy of life. When students become aware of the strengths of others, they also become aware of their own strengths. Pointing out positives can be foundational to an encouragement group.

- Separate the doer from the deed: "That behavior is not helpful to us, but you are!" The concept of encouragement is based on a foundation of existence-based acceptance, not just recognition for positive behavior. When individuals are able to see themselves in a positive manner, separate from any negative incident that might have happened, it gives them the opportunity to accept imperfection and renewed energy to learn from their mistakes. Students are then able to focus on the behavioral infraction rather than the authority figure dealing with the misbehavior.
- Comment on the person's effort, not just the results: "I can see how hard you are trying." The emphasis of the observer is placed on the phrase "I can see." The recipient of the phrase will naturally feel noticed. The comment also energizes the individual to continue showing genuine effort.
- Instill the idea that mistakes can be a learning experience: "Let's discuss what we can learn from this mistaken choice." This is a statement of continued inclusion. The word *we* is key; it communicates the notion that students are equals in terms of dignity and respect. It also communicates the notion that students and teachers will remain together for the long haul.

Students who bully are discouraged about their relationship with others. Their faulty logic leads them to compensate by showing superiority in the form of power. Most schools have developed a zero-tolerance policy for physical bullying. Students are usually expelled for a period of time. It is the hope of school district officials that the suspension will deter the child from the choice to bully.

For some students, this might work. For others, a deeper problem exists. Therefore, it is extremely important to welcome students back when they return, making sure they are involved in the life of the school again. Prolonged isolation will only reinforce a child or adolescent's mistaken choice to seek power and revenge.

Expulsion from school for bullying is not primarily an individual problem. It is a social issue. Any form of misbehavior cannot be extracted from the social setting in which it occurred.

Bullying sometimes has to do with a generational family model of abuse. It might be a mistaken approach to life that states, "I must always win, or I must control others." It could be an angry firstborn child hopelessly dethroned by a second child, a squeezed middle-born struggling to find a place of belonging, or a last-born child who is continuously rescued from consequences. A lack of desire to contribute to the life of others—social interest—is the major influence.

Students who bully are deeply discouraged and in desperate need of encouragement. Other students can be a primary source of needed encouragement and can provide both short-term and long-term motivation for students who bully to show cooperation.

FORMING ENCOURAGEMENT GROUPS

Students are fully capable of becoming encouraging people. They can be instruments of encouragement to other students. When a student is discouraged, other students instinctively want to participate in the helping process. In the example in chapter 4, a teacher asked the class, "How many of you would be willing to help Stephen?" Every hand was raised with insightful ideas to encourage him.

Encouragement groups exist for the purpose of contributing to the emotional well-being of the students involved in the group. The group provides a setting where fellow students can share experiences that are challenging to them: feelings of less-than, difficulties with social adjustment, negative encounters with other students or teachers, family issues, academic problems, and myriad other challenges. Acceptance, belonging, and encouragement are foundational in the group.

When a discouraged student communicates a personal struggle, other members can provide encouragement. Students who remain discouraged will become competitive and will eventually show extreme contempt toward others In the words of Dreikurs (2000), "Discouragement is at the root of all misbehavior" (p. 10). As discouragement subsides, violent behavior will do the same. *Encouragement groups can be a useful tool in eliminating school shootings and other forms of violent behavior. Members of encouragement groups can provide deeply discouraged students with significance and purpose.*

Students in an encouragement group can discuss the four mistaken goals of behavior. Attention-getting mechanisms can elicit humor, especially when group members share them in the context of childhood. Group members will have stories about power struggles with parents, teachers, and coaches and how they were resolved. Individuals in the group can share strategies they used to deal with feelings of anger that might have become a motive for revenge. *Children and adolescents can solve issues related to the four mistaken goals of behavior in the encouragement group.*

Perceptions of less-than continually intimidate us. Encouragement groups can help individuals deal with the feelings of inferiority. Inferiority is the belief that we are not as good as others. These feelings can lead to insecurity, which often results in reactions of defensiveness or anxiety. Feelings of inadequacy can also impede the desire to cooperate with fellow students. Members of an encouragement group can point out strengths in one another. *Children in encouragement groups are viewed by each student in the group as important and valuable!*

Encouragement groups help new students make immediate contact with existing students. Generally speaking, the anxiety of a new student is communicated in the questions: Will I make friends? Will I be accepted? What will I be known for? For adults, the answers to these questions will not drift a great distance from a previously established approach to life. Elementary and high school students on the other hand, are still attempting to fine-tune the answers to these questions. *Encouragement groups can help reduce the angst of being a new student and enhance new students' sense of belonging.*

Encouragement groups can eliminate students' desire to bully through the development of social interest. Encouragement groups aid the development of social interest by showing acceptance of others regardless of their imperfections. Each member will reciprocate the empathy that is inherent in the group. *Those who have been bullied can receive useful information from others who have had the same experience.*

Adler defined social interest as community feeling. This can be the within encouragement group as well as in the larger community. Commitment to members of the group is an act of social interest. Involvement in an encouragement group naturally gives members a healthy amount of recognition. Social interest is a learned behavior; however, it must be nurtured. Social interest helps the individual discover that all people are interdependent; the welfare of one individual affects the welfare of other individuals. The act of encouraging fellow students is a practical example of this concept. *An encouragement group can commit to encourage others who might be struggling.*

Social interest encompasses interconnectedness, which is vital for living together effectively in society. Social interest contributes to the healthy development of all individuals. Young babies require the emotional connections of parents and caregivers or they will struggle both physically and emotionally. The greater one's personal development, the greater the chance that individual can connect with others, learn from them, encourage them, and become encouraged by them. *Encouragement groups can accomplish this.*

Encouragement group members eventually begin to share at a deeper level as individual members begin to understand that others have similar challenges in hurtful circumstances. Members develop empathy and can provide support as well as practical ways to solve everyday problems. *When students—or adults, for that matter—come to the realization that others have problems similar to their own, they are more energized to solve them in useful ways.*

Encouragement groups can be vital in helping students deal with perfectionism and the relentless striving it creates. Adler (1956) noted that "we shall always find in human beings this great line of activity—this struggle to rise from an inferior to a superior position, from defeat to victory, from below to above. It begins in earliest childhood and continues to the end of our lives" (p. 103).

Perfectionism can lead to many unnecessary problems in life. Lombardi (1991) lists what he labels pitfalls; each of these creates difficult behavior:

- *Excel at any cost*, which involves the notion of doing whatever it takes, regardless of how it might affect others, in order to reach the perfectionist goal.
- *Futility/do nothing* can lead a person to a sense of uselessness, resulting in complete inactivity. The individual simply becomes listless and inactive.
- *Conceal at any costs* is a behavior of many strategies. The perfectionist attempts to hide, makes excuses, creates alibis, lies, and blames others, with the ultimate goal of protecting self-esteem.
- *The jitters* create anxiety, nervousness, and agitation.

Encouragement groups can deal with these challenges, which also contributes to the emotional health of each member.

Encouragement groups enhance the feeling of usefulness in children and adolescents. When children or high school students feel useful, they naturally stay encouraged and contribute to others in encouraging ways. Feeling useful is vital! *Group members can discuss encouragement skills to create their own sense of usefulness.*

The farming and ranching era of the past provided a much easier paradigm for the development of responsibility, since children were vital to family survival. As soon as a child was able to walk with some degree of strength and coordination, chores were assigned, often with economic consequences attached. Daily chores might be related to nurturing newborn lambs, spreading feed to chickens, and milking cows. Each of these chores was inherently important to the farm's sustainability. Children intrinsically knew that farm production would be affected in significant ways if they did not complete the necessary tasks.

Learning to solve everyday problems in a constructive manner is an important topic for encouragement groups. For children and adolescents, developing problem-solving skills builds self-confidence and interdependence. Adler identified life tasks that are significant: contribution to society, love, self-development, and spirituality. Group members can define these and can talk about their role in developing their life plans.

Encouragement group participants keep tabs on one another. When a group member has missed school, a text or phone call of concern can be made. Students can be taught to look for behavior that concerns them. Comments showing anger, obvious facial countenance, spontaneous moodiness, fixation on guns or other instruments of violence, and any mention of any form of violence in Twitter or Facebook posts would be important to note. If this were the case, a person in authority should be immediately contacted.

Psychiatrists sometimes use the term *brain wiring*. Defining brain wiring is somewhat complicated because it is full of medical terminology. Simply paraphrased, it has to do with damage or wounds to a neuron through emotional or physical harm. Positive comments contribute to the prevention of damage to brain neurons. Physical protection, such as a football helmet, can protect neurons from physical damage. Damaged neurons can contribute to inhibitory or excitable actions in brain function. Although the research is fairly recent, new theories of emotional abuse, juxtaposed to reward and satisfaction, have been found to contribute to the regulation of emotions. *Encouragement groups can make helpful contributions to the positive side of brain wiring.*

Encouragement groups can discuss various strategies for changing patterns of misbehavior. One plan of action might be to *act as if.* In this technique, members can try out new roles and creative ways to deal with impending issues. *Catching oneself* is helpful in identifying behaviors that are still in need of change. Constructive ways of changing behavior can follow once the repeated behavior has been identified. "What would be different if you . . . ?" and "Where do you think this is headed?" are insightful questions to ask.

Members can also exaggerate a challenge they are facing and then ask the question, "What would be so awful about . . . if that really happened?" A similar question might be: "When something like that changed, what would really be different?" Would you, for example, still have to put gas in your car; change a faulty electrical cord if it was shorting out your video game; drink water; or check your cell phone for texts?

Most behavior, whether negative or positive, is not premeditated. School shootings are premeditated and therefore are an act of revenge. Other behavior is less conscience, and simply needs to be pointed out. The aforementioned questions can be helpful in identifying negative behavior choices. Encouragement group members can point out both negative and positive behavior choices. The questions are meant to enhance discussions about less conscious behavior.

In many locations throughout the United States, high schools are experimenting with a small-group program that involves the use of high school students to deal with disciplinary actions. The program is called restorative justice.

One unique aspect of this approach is that both the perpetrator and the victim are a part of the small group. The program is relatively new, but educators are taking a serious look at it. At the present time, the rates of recidivism in schools that use restorative justice are lower than with standard disciplinary actions. Kathy Evans (Vaandering & Evans, 2016) of Eastern Mennonite University writes, "Engage children and youth. . . . When they are given opportunities and support to take on leadership roles, they have the potential to deeply strengthen the culture of the school" (p. 108).

Training teachers to detect mental health issues in a student's life is also important and vital. Including student members of encouragement groups, however, increases the number of eyes and ears exponentially. *The talent, enthusiasm, and creativity evidenced in the movement on Washington, DC, leaves little doubt that students can figure out a way to enroll all the children in any given school into an encouragement group.*

SUICIDE

According to the Centers for Disease Control and Prevention (CDC, 2011), suicide is the second-leading cause of preventable death among young people between the ages of fifteen and twenty-four. Only accidents and cancer rate higher. Experts in suicidology list important factors that can influence students to take their lives.

According to Dr. Mary Geffen, relatively few poor teenagers take their own lives. According to her research, middle- and upper-class teenagers are the most vulnerable. This particular group of students is generally successful in school activities. The risk they face comes when the status they have attained is threatened. When things go awry, they seem to lack the ability to solve the issues at hand. Geffen states that the "too-perfect child may be at a greater risk of suicide. A tumble from his excessively high standards and expectations may leave him feeling worthless" (*Changing Times*, 1982).

Geffen lists other risk factors for young people, including feeling that life is a series of failures, dropping out of high school, lacking meaningful social relationships, feeling that one has no promising future, having no sense of contributing, and and being rejected socially. Walton (1988) gives additional perspective, stating that "when young people who have learned to think their very worth is dependent upon meeting some achievement standard, or upon avoiding criticism, and believe they are falling short of these objectives, they may choose suicide as a method of *revenge* or *escape*" (p. 184).

Walton continues by listing another posibility: overambitious pampering and coercive parenting styles. With regard to revenge, the person feels mistreated by loved ones. Rather than attempting to find a practical solution, the individual desires to inflict the greatest hurt possible: suicide.

Both of these parenting styles are detrimental. Children who are pampered rarely learn to solve problems. Parents take the initiative to solve the issue before the pampered child has a chance to be a part of the solving process. Children who are forced to behave in certain ways do not experience the value of experiencing logical and natural consequences. A feeling of uselessness and worthlessness can set in, leading to suicide.

The interpersonal theory of suicide (Joiner, 2005) suggests that suicidal behavior is influenced when a person has both a desire to take their life and the capacity to do so. The individual perceives that he or she is a burden and also feels a great deal of social alienation.

In 1937 Adler wrote about suicide in relation to the degree of social isolation and feelings of inferiority that an individual perceived. Mistaken beliefs and faulty private logic (behavior that an individual is not fully aware of until it is pointed out) were also factors. Adler was firm about the fact that suicide was complicated. Adler believed that suicide made sense only to individuals who were at the end of a limited amount of social interest and were confronted with a problem they perceived as insurmountable.

A Brief Story of Courtney and Her Close Call with Death by Suicide

Courtney was the third girl in a family of four siblings; the fourth child was a boy. When she was a sophomore in high school, she came dangerously close to death when she overdosed on Tylenol. After swallowing a significant number of the pills, she panicked and told her mother. She was rushed to the hospital, where lifesaving procedures were performed. Forty-five minutes had elapsed since she ingested the pills; one hour puts the person in an extremely vulnerable condition.

My two older sisters were always competing for the attention of my parents. They argued all the time. Sometimes they even pushed and shoved. My brother was like a prince. He never got in trouble. Somehow, he convinced my older sister to do all his chores. Mostly, I felt like I didn't fit. I was just there. We were all about fifteen months apart.

I tried lots of things, but failed to get my parents' approval. I tried out for cheer, but didn't make it like my sisters did. I played the saxophone and tried to make the jazz ensemble, but I wasn't chosen. Most of my friends were getting boyfriends, but I didn't think any boys were really that interested in me. When I joined drama, I was only selected to paint the backdrops. I was pretty good in art so I guess that was kind of a success for me, but my parents didn't make much of a big deal out of it.

I had a few friends. I liked them, and I think they liked me. The problem was they were good at stuff, and I wasn't that good at anything. Finally, after being cut from softball tryouts, I just gave up. I said to myself, "I quit." After crying for about an hour, I poured a whole bunch of Tylenols into both hands and swallowed them. I did it twice. I went back to my room, realized what I had done, and told my mom. She called 911, and I spent a few days in the hospital and a week living at a therapy place. I guess I just didn't know how to live without being good at something. (Personal interview)

Courtney appears to be from a middle- or upper middle-class family; both cheerleading and saxophone are activities involving a not insignificant financial investment, and her school provided access to drama and sports teams.

Rather than facing the discouragement that was confronting her or dealing with further criticism, Courtney attempted to end her life. Some individuals, rather than dealing with the difficulties of life, would rather escape it by taking their own lives. They lack a firm belief in their ability to tolerate emotional distress in life. *An encouragement group could help indviduals develop more resilience.*

Courtney had friends with whom she would spend time; she was not in danger of complete social rejection. Her personal narrative gives no indication of academic issues. She perceived a definite need for approval from her parents that contributed to her exaggerated desire for success in order to gain that approval. She does, however, fit the profile of a teenager who experienced one failure after another.

It is important to note that it wasn't her lack of success that drained her energy to go on; rather, it was the meaning she attached to it. She mistakenly perceived it as a general failure in life itself. Her approach to life—what Adler called lifestyle—is probably something similar to, "In order to feel important and valuable in my parents' eyes, I must be successful at something."

We have no evidence of pampering toward her youngest brother. According to Courtney, her younger brother could have been on the receiving end of that particular method of parenting. Her birth order position did seem to be a factor according to the way she interpreted the situation. Family constellation dynamics were challenging for her. Her two older sisters fought constantly, sometimes resulting in physical altercations. Her second-born sister undoubtedly was not willing to take a subordinate position to her oldest sister.

The constant fighting between her older sisters probably preoccupied her parents, preventing the younger two children from receiving a share of the attention. However, she described her youngest brother as a "prince" who managed to manipulate her oldest sister into completing his chores. It is likely that Courtney's three siblings were collectively successful at sucking all of the attention out of the room. According to Courtney's perception, a place of belonging—or perhaps even a potential place of belonging—was nonexistent. Her earliest recollections had to do with hearing her parents talking about the successes of other people. It is likely that she interpreted success as a family value.

In order for Courtney to develop self-encouragement strategies to deal with the defeats she was experiencing, it would have been helpful for her parents, a teacher, or an encouragement group to point out her strengths.

It took a tremendous amount of courage to try out for all the activities she desired to compete in. Perhaps she fell short in the talent that was needed to earn a position on the teams, ensemble, or drama performances. However, her efforts were notable. She had a few friends whom she liked and who she thought liked her as well. Her social interest was at least partially developed. She was able to focus on her studies well enough to maintain adequate grades throughout her disappointments, which is a definite positive.

It seems that Courtney simply grew weary of trying to please her parents—and, to a certain extent, herself. Even though her logic was faulty, which needed to be respectfully pointed out to her, she still had many positives going for her. *Involvement in an encouragement group can be important for adolescents like Courtney. Undoubtedly, other participants would share similar observations and experiences about their own parents.*

A Brief Story about Nick, a Socially Awkward Student

Fisher (1987) examines the sad account of a socially confused boy. His cries for help were heard, but no one responded in ways that might have prevented his suicide. As has been stated throughout this chapter, the underlying human need is to experience a place of belonging. Negative behavior is often the result of a lack of knowledge about how to show positive behavior that helps one find a place to belong. Nick's last day of life gives insight into how well or poorly he was able to participate with others. He desired social significance. He was just not sure how to achieve it. Although he sometimes showed constructive acts toward others, he was still labeled as socially awkward.

On March 26, 1987, the *Washington Post* published a story titled "A Student's 'Goodbye' Suicide Shocks D.C. Junior High School." The story that unfolds is disheartening, confusing, and shocking. Nick Linenberger was a sixteen-year-old junior high student who wanted just one thing in life: to be a part of the crowd. On his last day at school, he made an obvious gesture, sticking out his hand and shouting, "Goodbye!" The teacher he was attempting to contact was busy with someone else. He was so insistent that the teacher finally walked over to greet him.

LaVerne Bass, a teacher and coach, said, "The boy insisted, standing there with his arm extended, saying 'good-bye' again and again" (Qtd. in Fisher, 1987). She mentioned that Nick often came around in the afternoons just to talk or help her if she needed it. He was known to encourage teachers when he sensed they were down. He painted a portrait of Martin Luther King

Jr. and sang a solo of "Swing Low, Sweet Chariot," receiving numerous accolades.

His mother described him as a distressed boy "who very much wanted to be a part of the in-crowd, a troubled child who struggled in academics and excelled in extracurricular activities" (Fisher, 1987). His dad, who was in the military, was previously stationed in Belgium. When they were relocated, Nick enrolled at Hart Junior High School in Congress Heights. He was only one of six white students out of one thousand minority students. Apparently, it was a difficult time of adjustment for him, but he eventually began to fit in.

The positive contributions that Nick left his fellow students were numerous. Besides consoling teachers, painting a portrait of King, and singing "Swing Low, Sweet Chariot," in his Latin class he also drew a copy of a bronze coin depicting black soldiers in Hannibal's army.

After his death, his classmates expressed varied forms of grief. The student newspaper did a front-page feature on him. His painting was moved to the auditorium. His portrait of the coin was placed on the wall, bordered in black, so students could sign it under the verbiage "Rest in Peace." Another student asked students and teachers to sign a banner that read, "God be with you, Nick." Teachers stood in the hallways crying and telling stories—both positive and negative—about him.

Nick was known for kind gestures, but he was also troubled. He could kindly hug a teacher one moment and start a fight with a student the next moment. He was banned from riding the school bus for playing with matches. He hated to do his homework. He would get into fights just looking for attention. Nick had a problem with stealing, and the day before his death he was in a fight next to the ice cream truck. When talking about Nick a few days after his death, his mom stated, "He was so confused."

Nick was clearly misunderstood. According to the school's principal, "Nick didn't seem any different from any other child at Hart. We had no idea that he was encountering problems of that magnitude. That's the tragic problem facing our teenagers today. They need to express their feelings, to turn to someone with their problems." Bass reflected, "You come in every day, and you know children have problems just like adults. But to detect that Nick was ready to take his life, I just can't imagine it. I can't imagine he did it" (Qtd. in Fisher, 1987).

Mental health experts, school officials, parents, and friends were in total bewilderment at Nick's act of suicide. What were the clues, hints, or statements that illustrated the psychological state of this young student? What was the purpose or reason for the behavior of suicide?

Nick received positive remarks about his important contributions, yet he was unable to translate those comments into a feeling of acceptance. Perhaps his incidents of negative behavior had influenced his perception. Very little is mentioned about his father. Possibly a dynamic—positive or negative—was at play in his relationship with his father. Perhaps the medical community would posit that Nick was chemically depressed. All would agree that Nick needed a venue to share his feelings at a deeper level. *Involvement in an encouragement group could have been the setting that made a difference in his level of support.*

EATING DISORDERS

Melissa and Her Experience with an Eating Disorder

Eating disorders represent another concern among school personnel, parents, and health professionals. Perfectionism, an exaggerated need for attention, and family dysfunction can all contribute to eating disorders.

Melissa was born into a family of three children. She was the middle-born child with an older sister and a younger one.

> I was given to my older sister as if she was my real mom. The difficulty was that she seemed to do everything in a perfect way. She was responsible, always following through on what she was asked to do. Worst of all, she was the perfect weight, very popular and got outstanding grades.
>
> I remember lying awake at night, sometimes crying, because I just didn't know where I fit in. My sister was known for just about everything. I wasn't sure I was known for anything. It was a terrible feeling. When my sister got her period, she put on weight. She wasn't perfect anymore. My youngest sister just smiled and laughed all the time. Every kid liked her.
>
> I decided to stop eating. This was my chance to be something she no longer was. It was easier than I thought, at least at first. I started losing weight. The attention was unbelievable. My sister started getting in a little more trouble than before, so I went opposite of her behavior. My parents seemed totally confused. I guess I was too, but it really felt good.
>
> I really started losing weight. Food made me sick. All of a sudden, the attention was all negative. I couldn't help myself. Everyone started yelling at me, even doctors and especially my parents.
>
> Then, a miracle happened. I guess it was a miracle. We are not religious people, so I am not exactly sure what a miracle really is. That's what the school counselor called it. I noticed a girl at school. She was sitting alone, crying at lunch like I used to do. Every day she was alone.
>
> I finally asked her why she was always crying. She didn't even look up. She said, if she didn't start eating more, she would have to go to the hospital and probably lose what few friends she had left. I knew how she felt. I started crying. She looked up at me. I told her I had the same problem. We agreed to start texting. We also agreed to try to start to eat more. Because we had each other, being noticed wasn't as important as before.
>
> The school counselor called us in one day and asked whether another student, who also had eating problems, could join us. She was different. She would eat too much and then throw up. We didn't know anything about that.

One thing we did agree on was that attention wasn't as important as we thought. I guess we moved past it. We did it together. It was a lot easier that way. (Personal interview)

The influences and causes of eating disorders are many and varied. The early psychoanalytic model expressed a separation-individuation trauma resulting in a fear of maturation (Bruch, 1973). Cognitive behaviorists theorized that a faulty belief system about thinness and inadequacy was at fault (Vitousek & Hollon, 1990). Society's messages about the thin ideal is foundational to sociocultural theory (Wiseman, Gray, Mosimann, & Ahrens, 1992). Adlerian theory holds to the notion that eating disorders are mistaken goals of perfectionism. A study done by Egan, Wade, and Saharan (2010) discovered that perfectionism maintained high levels of motivation in the cycle of mistaken perceptions about weight.

Melissa mistakenly interpreted that her sister's popularity was based on perfectionist behavior patterns. Her mistaken approach to life could be summed up in the self-talk statement, "In order to feel important and valuable, I must be perfect." Her eating disorder can be attributed to her cycle or pattern of perfectionist thought patterns leading to becoming the perfect weight.

An erroneous belief about the self becomes intertwined with the child's view of how one attains love, value, belonging, and acceptance in a family that overvalues appearance. The child is likely to have a strong desire to please parents, teachers, and peers. In the process, however, this child loses important aspects of social interest.

Social interest, as explained earlier in this chapter, is community interest that moves toward positive connections with others. Eating disorders are selfish in nature. People struggling with eating disorders are self-absorbed in the sense that the focus of their attention is entirely on themselves. Individuals with eating disorders lose valuable associations that could enhance belonging and acceptance.

Melissa was unable to establish a sense of importance apart from her sister, who was on her own journey of perfectionism. Appearance seems to be an important family value supported by both parents. Melissa's sister was so perfect that she could easily fulfill the role of a surrogate mother. Both parents were convinced that the most efficient way to perpetuate the family value of appearance was to let their perfect oldest daughter have a formidable influence on Melissa. Her earliest recollection is the memory of her mom's excitement every time her movie star magazine came in the mail.

Adler (1956), when describing the second child, states, "Throughout his childhood . . . there is always a child ahead of him, and he is stimulated to exert himself and catch up" (p. 379). Typical of a second child, Melissa was intently waiting to dethrone her "perfect" older sister. When Melissa observed that her sister was putting on weight, she quickly acted. Melissa, at least according to her perception, became the important child in the family. She discovered, however, it wasn't exactly what she imagined. This was a mature viewpoint that she learned from a logical consequence, perhaps because she had experienced both sides of a mistaken perception.

Social interest is a learned behavior. Griffith and Powers (2007) follow up on that idea, stating that it is a "universal capacity," but it does require fostering and nurturing, similar to the development of language and speech. Melissa awakened her social interest when she reached out to the girl who was crying during lunch. A key word associated with social interest is *empathy*. Melissa and her new friend formed an encouragement group. The group increased by one member when the school counselor asked Melissa to invite another person.

BULLYING

Nathaniel's Bullying Experiences

Nathaniel was a freshman in high school and was considered quiet. He was not a problem in school. He almost always had his homework done, and his grades were above average. His parents were concerned about his social life. He didn't seem to have any friends, and teachers reported that he spent most of his lunches alone. His social problems increased significantly after he developed a severe case of acne. He was criticized verbally, and varied forms of bullying from others increased.

His parents also reported that he was called "awful" names. He fought back by avoiding people. He even created hideouts at school to eat his lunch—places where no one could find him. His parents became concerned when he began using hateful language about others at school.

> I was an only child so I didn't mind spending time alone. It had always been that way, anyway. I never felt like I had anything that important to say to most people. Sometimes, I was lonely, but there were always kids online to play internet games. Sometimes they were the same kids, but many times they weren't. I wouldn't call them friends, just people who enjoyed the same games.
>
> My dislike for other people started when my face developed pimples and I was made fun of. I was no different than when I didn't have pimples. I was quiet, and others left me alone. Then, people noticed me. I was called "leprosy face, pimple boy, acne king and others." I started staying away from everyone.
>
> I even had hiding places at school when I wasn't in class. Some days, I would clench my fists and cry all the way home. My parents would say, "Stand up to them," but how? If they didn't beat me up physically, the name-calling

would be worse. I remember thinking of ways to get back at them. But how? I thought about suicide.

My only hope was the strong medicine the doctor gave me. She said it would take three to six months and my face would probably get better. With only three months of school remaining and two months of summer, maybe I could make it. I was really down.

I guess the heroes were the medicine and my "Nanna." She read about a program that was going on in the summer. It was for kids who had an interest in robots. I was good at taking things apart just to see how they worked. The garage was full of junk from my projects. I was afraid to go because of my face. My "Nanna" made me go. My face was doing better.

There were about eight kids who came. We started putting together robots from kits that they gave us. I guess I was pretty good at it. Other kids asked me to help them. We became friends. The teacher asked me to be in the robot club at school.

When school started, my face looked pretty normal. In December, our club got to go to be in a national contest. We finished eighth in the country. My name was read over the loudspeaker with the others. It was the last time I was made fun of, and I had friends. The school counselor asks me to invite other kids who were being made fun of to be in our club. They usually say yes. (Personal interview)

Nathaniel was in a precarious situation. He chose to live on the quieter side of life and appeared not to misuse his apparent introversion for manipulative purposes. He got decent grades, completed his homework, and was not a problem at school. His parents were concerned about lack of social life, which probably says more about their values than about his social position. Perhaps his birth order position as an only child was a factor in his contentment at being alone. Although he doesn't mention it, he might have considered himself to be socially awkward.

The difficult situation was the reality that he had no one to support him in surviving the excruciating experience of being bullied. It would be accurate to say he had a few acquaintances at school; otherwise, he would probably have experienced truancy issues. He simply had no one close enough to encourage him. He was a definite candidate for an encouragement group. In actuality, it was his membership in the robot club—a group association—that became his source of survival and encouragement. His doctor was also helpful in prescribing the proper medication for his acne issues.

Nathaniel had a natural curiosity to learn. His earliest recollection was watching a high school neighbor working on his car "all the time." The garage was full of "junk" from his projects. He enjoyed taking things a part just to see how they were supposed to work. It was not his intention to learn how certain things worked in order to get a grade, perform well on a test, or to show off his mechanical skill. Nathaniel was also creative. He found places to hide when he knew others were looking for him. No doubt it was a painful experience to lose the opportunity to meet other students at lunch or to simply people watch. His practical side was also operational: "It doesn't make any sense to be around people who want to hurt you."

Probably his deepest hurt had something to do with this: "My dislike for other people started when my face developed pimples and I was made fun of. I was no different than when I didn't have pimples. I was quiet and others left me alone." Perhaps for the first time, Nathaniel experienced the cruel side of humanity. He started to despise the kids whom he once respected, at least from a distance. That is not to say the words didn't hurt. He remembered them word for word. I am sure they stung!

Regardless of the pressure from his Nanna, it took courage to attend the robot classes. First of all, his acne wasn't completely cleared up, and second, what if one or two of the kids who teased him were in attendance as well? Nathaniel did quite well in the robot classes. Perhaps he had some natural talent in electronic and mechanical subject areas, or perhaps in his time alone he had learned and honed his skills about why things worked or didn't work.

Despite the mistreatment of his peers, Nathaniel maintained his social interest. He invited fellow students who were struggling to join the robot club. He had no experience with an encouragement group prior to his efforts in the robot class, but he somehow reached deep into his creative self and endured his circumstances. He was clearly practical, wise, and courageous, and enjoyed learning for the sake of learning. Adler, among the aggressive scientific psychologists of his era, stood firm with his belief in the creative self, developing a psychology of the soul. Adler (1964) wrote, "We have been impelled to attribute to the child a creative power . . . a movement toward the overcoming of an obstacle" (p. 177).

In Nathaniel's personal narrative, he mentions the advice from his parents to stand up to the students who were tormenting him. He was realistic in his viewpoint about the futility of that particular strategy. He knew that a physical altercation would only create more chaos. He did note, however, that he considered ways to retaliate against the students who were bothering him. He came to the conclusion that it wasn't practical.

Once again, he was realistic when he asked, "But how?" His other expression of desperation is revealed when he mentions he considered suicide. He uses the phrases, "I thought about suicide . . . my only hope. . . . I was really down." Due to his situation, it would be unrealistic to think that the thought of escape through suicide had not crossed his mind.

Nathaniel was able to overcome his challenging situation. He was patient and activated his skills. But it is possible that if Nathaniel had access to a gun, the result would have been tragic.

SCHOOL SHOOTINGS

A brief history of school-related shootings reinforces the need for encouragement groups. The loss of life from twenty-two school shootings halfway through 2018 is difficult to comprehend. The following are just a few of them. Not all shootings have taken place on school campuses, and not all shootings were carried out by students at the school.

> *May 25, Noblesville, Indiana:* Two people were injured when a gunman opened fire at Noblesville West Middle School.
>
> *May 18, Santa Fe, Texas:* Ten people were killed in a shooting at Santa Fe High School.
>
> *May 11, Palmdale, California:* A fourteen-year-old boy went to Highland High, his former school, and began shooting a semiautomatic rifle shortly before classes were scheduled to begin, officials said. A fifteen-year-old boy was struck in the shoulder.
>
> *April 12, Raytown, Missouri:* A man was shot in the stomach in the parking lot of Raytown South Middle School during a track meet.
>
> *March 20, Lexington Park, Maryland:* An armed student shot two others at Great Mills High School before a school resource officer fired a round at the shooter. The shooter was killed. One of the students, sixteen-year-old Jaelynn Willey, was taken off life support two days later.
>
> *February 14, Parkland, Florida:* A nineteen-year-old former student gunned down students and staff with a rifle at Marjory Stoneman Douglas High School in Parkland, killing seventeen unsuspecting students and adults. The shooter, Nikolas Cruz, had been expelled from the high school over disciplinary problems, officials said.
>
> *February 9, Nashville, Tennessee:* A high school student was shot five times in the parking lot of Pearl-Cohen High School.
>
> *January 23, Benton, Kentucky:* A fifteen-year-old student shot sixteen people—killing two other fifteen-year-olds—at Marshall County High School, authorities said. The student faces two charges of murder and twelve counts of first-degree assault.
>
> *January 22, Italy, Texas:* A fifteen-year-old student was wounded in a shooting at a high school in Italy, Texas, authorities said. The suspect, also fifteen, was quickly apprehended. (Saeed & Walker, 2018).

Encouragement groups can be useful in helping students overcome many challenges. *The most urgent one is to eliminate potential school shootings.* However, students face many serious issues, including suicide, eating disorders, drug addiction, poor academic performance, cooperation with others, and many other challenges. School shootings are painfully unforgettable, but so are suicides. Suicide is the second-leading cause of death among young people.

In the article "Law Enforcement Wasn't the First to Fail in the Parkland School Shooting," Maxwell (2018), provides insight into the school shooting crisis in Parkland, Florida, pointing out that numerous resources were in effect prior to the shooting: "school counselors, psychologists, . . . consultants, lawyers, networks of alternative schools to serve the so-called at-risk students." Nonetheless, students still become disenfranchised, resulting in "destructive actions."

The article describes some of the challenges Nikolas Cruz faced in his life prior to the shooting rampage. He was diagnosed with autism and witnessed the death of his father from a heart attack when he was only five years old. He was also on the receiving end of bullying and humiliation, which was a catalyst to bouts of antisocial and violent behavior patterns.

Cruz experienced a two-year reprieve from the trauma when he was transferred to a school for special needs students. His behavior noticeably changed, with no violent outbursts, after he experienced a positive relationship with an industrial arts teacher.

Unfortunately, he was transferred back to the public school, where the cycle of teasing and bullying commenced again. Any significant personal improvement dissipated as he disappeared into thoughts of revenge. After his horrific acts of violence, school officials did remember more about him, but it was too late.

Other people besides school officials, were aware of the behavioral issues Cruz was dealing with. Rose and Booker (2018) relate that professionals in various specialties were aware that he was deeply troubled. According to police records, he was the subject of numerous 911 calls. Police were specifically alerted when he and his brother were involved in physical altercations. Cruz also came to the attention of the FBI and the Florida Department of Children and Families. Concern for Cruz began when he was ten years old. Deputies reported eighteen separate incidences involving Cruz prior to the Parkland shoting. Unfortunately, none of them mandated arrest.

After the family was forced to sell their house and Cruz's mother passed away, another alarming incident took place when he engaged in a fight with a member of the family he was staying with. Cruz began punching walls and put a gun to the person's head. He had apparently done that to his brother and his mother on previous occasions. Cruz was also known to self-harm, having posted photos of his self-harm on Snapchat.

There were still other precursors to the fatal shooting. A bail bondsman reported that someone—Cruz—had left a message in the comments section of a YouTube video stating, "I'm going to be a school shooter." A person close to Cruz mentioned that he had a "desire to kill people," and a caller to law enforcement officials believed that Cruz had the potential to conduct a school shooting. (Rose and Booker, 2018)

What if Cruz had been part of an encouragement group? Obviously, he was deeply disturbed and extremely desperate for some form of attention, significance, and positive interaction with other students. Participation in an encouragement group could have provided attention and support. Membership alone might have provided the recognition he was looking for.

Cruz was also deeply hurt, largely due to his feelings of inferiority and his perception that he was disliked by others. Unfortunately, he mistakenly believed that a planned act of revenge was his only way to fight back. *Encouragement groups can help adolescents deal with feelings of inferiority. The supportive nature of a group would have helped Cruz deal with the teasing and bullying.*

Authorities reported that Cruz responded positively to an industrial arts teacher. He was capable, at that time, to receive and reciprocate positive behavioral actions. According to Adler (1956) "social interest which is inherent in every human society. The degree to which social interest is developed in a person, gives measures, not only to his desires, but even more of his actions" (p. 449). According to this principle, Cruz had developed at least some degree of social interest.

Rose and Booker (2018) also point out that Cruz had developed a few friendships that were intact at the time of the shooting. Although he was seen as a loner, "those who knew him considered him a friend." Ethan Trieu, a fellow student, said, "I can't wrap my head around it. You know, we would just talk to each other like any other friends, and I know, some other people, he'd talk to just fine also. And, I know, just seeing his name is just weird. I don't know."

The calamity that ensued at Marjory Stoneman Douglas High School might have been prevented through the existence of an encouragement group. Nickolas Cruz could have been supported by others in the group when he was bullied and teased; other students who had similar experiences would have been invaluable in sharing strategies with him.

Friends from his encouragement group could also have helped him with the loss of his mother and the grief associated with that loss. Following the loss of both parents, an encouragement group could have given him the camaraderie he might have found in a functional family. Undoubtedly, others in the group would have gone through similar experiences of grief.

Personality traits associated with school shooters are identified by O'Toole (1999) and the Diagnostic and Statistical Manual of Mental Disorders, 5th ed. (American Psychiatric Association, 2013). They are as follows:

- Poor tolerance for frustration and coping skills

- Lack of resilience, failed intimate relationship, perceived injustices, and depression, "narcissism," alienation, dehumanization of others
- Lack of empathy, exaggerated entitlement, superiority attitude, and need for attention (exaggerated or pathological)
- Externalized blame, low self-esteem masked, anger control issues, prejudice toward minorities
- Symptoms, "inappropriate humor," manipulation of others, and poor trust in others;
- Closed social group, dramatic behavior change, opinionated and rigid
- Unusual interest in sensational violence, fascination with violence-filled entertainment, and negative role models

The difficulty for mental health professionals is that this list also aligns with typical characteristics of oppositional defiant disorder (ODD), acting-out issues, and rebelliousness. Also, a particular behavior could be normal in one particular family, region, and culture but not in another. O'Toole (1999) also identified four traits of family dynamics that are common to an active shooter: lack of communication from the family, infrequent parent involvement, reputation masking, and privacy values.

Children with ODD are not typically school shooters. The tragedy at Parkland is that Nikolas Cruz somehow gained access to a rapid-fire rifle. The Oppositional Defiance Disorder was not the key factor as much as his access to the rifle.

On May 18, 2018, another deadly shooting took place at Santa Fe High School in Santa Fe, Texas. The shooter was Dimitrios Pagourtzis, a seventeen-year-old student who planned to commit suicide after killing his classmates. He opened fire, killing ten students, but lost his courage when he was faced with taking his own life. Before the shooting, he posted a picture of a T-shirt sporting the phrase "Born to Kill." The other hate rhetoric posted on his Facebook page included the phrases "Hammer and Sickle = Rebellion," and "Rising Sun = Kamikaze Tactics. Iron Cross = Bravery. Baphomet = Evil."

The language Pagourtzis used was concerning. However, his behavior and participation around school did not align with his posts on Facebook. He was an honor roll student, played defensive tackle on the football team, was viewed by an AP language arts teacher as bright, and participated in a national history contest. He was described as quiet, but not in an alarming way. There were no reported cases of bullying, although his oldest sister was bullied relentlessly when she attended the school and was transferred to another school. It is unclear whether Pagourtzis was influenced by his sister's experiences.

The only clues that Pagourtzis communicated appeared on his Facebook page. He was living two lives. When he was at school, he participated as a student with a reasonable amount of social interest. His athletic involvement required cooperation with coaches and players. As a student, a portion of his life tasks were centered in his studies. He was on the honor roll and participated in a history contest, which would have required a certain degree of courage. Perhaps he was looking for more attention and notoriety. The only obvious negative experience he had was a breakup with his girlfriend.

Very little information is given to us about Pagourtzis's relationship with his father, mother, or older sister. He acquired the guns he used from his father. It is unlikely his father knew he had the guns, but we don't know that for sure. A fellow student mentioned that Pagourtzis wasn't particularly athletic, but he was a hard worker.

Dreikurs wrote *Children the Challenge* in 1964; it has sold more than six hundred thousand copies. One of many pertinent themes centers on the capabilities of children. It was Dreikurs's belief that children become responsible only when we give them responsibility. Children and adolescents are fully capable of creating and maintaining encouragement groups. Dreikurs also believed that misbehaving children are discouraged children. The opposite of discouragement is encouragement. The whole purpose of an encouragement group is to provide a small-group setting where individuals have the opportunity to give and receive encouragement.

Dreikurs viewed children as equals in terms of dignity and respect, but not necessarily in terms of position and responsibility. Therefore, it was his notion that children should be treated with the same basic regard as any human being. When we allow children to participate in positions of responsibility, we show faith in them, which serves as an important encouragement tool that transmits to other children and adolescents as well.

SPECIFICS OF AN ENCOURAGEMENT GROUP

- In an age of emphasis on school performance, districts will have to review their respective mission statements. School districts with the phrase "students first" will likely give serious attention to setting up encouragement groups.
- Those who are under binding procedures to become a Blue Ribbon School, Winning School, Excelling School, and the like might have to become more creative if they are to include times for encouragement groups to meet. The groups need to meet every day.
- Approximately five to seven people per group is most helpful for the participants.
- Since myriad issues can be dealt with, group attendance needs to be mandatory. Hopefully, the groups could receive a designation for credit.

Schools could include it in a four-year requirement as a part of a comprehensive health curriculum. Breakout groups could be a part of the class.
- Confidentiality must be strictly maintained unless a plan to hurt oneself or others is shared in the group.
- School officials are encouraged to participate equally with students at any time.

Encouragement groups can be effective in dealing with issues that children and high school students face on a daily basis. When problems are solved before they reach crisis proportions, students will grow with resilience, self-confidence, and refreshed social interest. The foundation for the problem-solving process is the social interest developed in an encouragement group.

CONCLUSION

A Brief Story of an Unfair Choice

I think I have made my decision. It was a difficult one, and, yet, it wasn't as difficult as I thought it would be. Time would pass, some days lingering more than others, and some days speeding by at record time as if the minute arm of the clock was in a life-and-death race to overtake the other. The passing of time was important to me. The clock, protected from error by an unseen force in the universe and the calendar, would determine my span of life. Many people use numeric age, some use the age of relatives, and some make guesses on what doctors say, to determine how long they will live. But was does age mean anyway? It's helping me make my decision.

I don't think that far ahead. If I went missing from school for a period of time, the clocks would still be working. The seconds would tick, minutes would strike the next number, and a new hour would announce the predictable mass movement of students. Would the clock announce that I was missing? How long would it take? Would the records show a statistic or would someone become concerned? I concluded, at best; I would simply be a designation, of some sort, at least for a period of time. It's helping me with my decision.

If could find a friend, just one person . . . although I wish I had two. What is it about me? I look in the mirror, and I see normal: someone who looks average and dresses okay. I even have earbuds with my favorite music on a playlist. I am smaller, but not that small. A lot of kids aren't very tall. So why me? When I come around the corner, I see them. I don't know that much about hawks, but it seems like they are hawks, and I am a fieldmouse. They are ready to attack me. But why? Oh well, it's helping me with my decision.

I live with my grandmother. She is eighty-three. She is starting to lose weight, but moves around okay. My parents were killed in a car accident, along with my older sister. I was with a babysitter when the accident hap-pened. I was very young. I don't remember much, just all kinds of people crying. Maybe when I am alone, that is why I cry so easily. It's been a lonely life. I just wish I had a good friend, or maybe two.

I have a secret way to walk to school. It gives me more time to be alone before I get teased or bullied. It's beautiful—breathtaking is more like it. It is a scene of stability. The waves of the bay splash against rocks that have not moved for thousands of years. The noise is almost deafening. It blocks out my problems for as long as I am there. I stand on a cliff, and sometimes I can see boats on the horizon. The cliff is approximately a hundred feet from the rocks and the water, I think.

I often wish I was on one of the boats, regardless of where it's going. The cliff takes me out of the way, so I have to make up about twenty minutes. I try to show up about the time the bell rings. But the bullies find me anyway. My stomach fills with anxiety. What name will they call me? How hard will they shove me? How embarrassing will it be? It's no wonder kids don't want to be around me. Every day I get closer to my decision.

I have told the school officials about the bullying. They say it needs to happen in front of a teacher, otherwise, they can't really do anything. My grandmother says I should ignore them, but she doesn't know how hard that is to do. What is wrong with them? What is wrong with me? Oh well, my decision is getting closer. I found a sawed-off shotgun my grandpa owned. I also found his ammunition. My grandma doesn't know I found it. Now my decision is really close. I just need a strategy.

The cliff is beautiful this time of year. It has grass on it. Sometimes people jog by me. I wonder what life is like for them. Do they have friends? Were they bullied in school? I just wish I had someone to talk to, maybe two people. Today, I was shoved into a locker. They tried to lock me in it; no teachers saw it. I ran faster than I ever have before. I could hear kids laughing in the background.

I ran out the front door of the school. I didn't return to school. I know what my strategy will be. I cried quite a bit last night. It's time! I hid the gun under my coat. I headed for school, but first I wanted to see the cliff one more time. I wasn't sure which option I would choose. . . but it was time. . . . The clock continued to click. . . . The waves splashed against the rocks. . . . The bullies were waiting. . . .

References

Adler, A. (1931) *What life should mean to you*. Boston, MA: Little, Brown.

Adler, A. (1937). Suicide. *International Journal of Individual Psychology*, *15*, 49–52.

Adler, A. (1956). *The Individual Psychology of Alfred Adler*. H. L. Ansbacher & R. R. Ansbacher, Eds. New York: Basic Books. 103.

Adler, A. (1963). *The problem child*. New York, NY: Putman's.

Adler, A. (1964). *The individual psychology of Alfred Adler: A systematic presentation in selections from his writings*. H. L. Ansbacher & Rowena R. Ansbacher (Eds.). New York, NY: Harper & Row.

Adler, A. (1969). *The education of children*. New York, NY: Greenberg.

Adler, A. (1998). *Understanding human nature*. (C. Brett, Trans.). Center City, MN: Hazelton.

Ahmed, S. and Walker, C. (2018) There has been, on average, 1 school shooting every week this year. May 25. CNN. http://www.cnn.com/2018/03/02/us/school-shootings-2018-list-trnd.html.

Ambrose, S. (1998). *Undaunted courage*. New York, NY: Simon & Schuster.

Anthony, S. (1859). Letter to the readers of the national anti-slavery standard. In Ann B. Gordon (Ed.), *The selected papers of Elizabeth Cady Stanton and Susan B. Anthony* (1: 385–86). New Brunswick, NJ: Rutgers University Press.

Ansbacher, H. L., & Ansbacher, R. R. (Eds.). (1956a). *The individual psychology of Alfred Adler*. New York, NY: Basic Books.

Ansbacher, H. L., & Ansbacher, R. R. (Eds.). (1956b). *Alfred Adler: Superiority and social interest*. New York, NY: Norton.

Anthony, S. (1859). Letter to the readers of the national anti-slavery standard (Ed.). *The Selected Papers of Elizabeth Cady Stanton and Susan B. Anthony*. (Ed.). Ann B. Gordon. New Jersey: Rutgers University Press, 161.

Attie, I., & Brooks-Gunn, J. (1987). Weight concerns as chronic overstress in women. In R. C. Barnett, L. Biener, & G. K. Baruch (Eds.), *Gender and stress* (219–54). New York, NY: Free Press.

Baumeister, R. F., & Leary, M. R. (1995). The need to belong: Desire for interpersonal attachments as a fundamental human motivation. *Psychological Bulletin*, *117*(3), 497, 529.

Bortoletti, S. C. (1999). *Kids on strike*. Boston, MA: Houghton Mifflin, 31–33.

Beemyn, B. G. (2005). Student organizations. glbtq: an encyclopedia of gay, lesbian, bisexual, transgender and queer culture. Retrieved from http://www.glbtqarchive.com/ssh/student_organizations_S.pdf.

Benson L., Harkavy I., & Puckett J. (2007). *Dewey's Dream*. Philadelphia, PA: Temple University Press.

Bruch, H. (1973). *Eating disorder: Obesity, anorexia nervosa and the person within.* New York, NY: Basic Books.

Brandt, K. M, S. J. (1997). *Story as a way of knowing.* Kansas City, MO: Sheed & Ward.

Brodhagen, B. L. (1995). The situation made us special. In M. W. Beane & J. Apple (Eds.), *Democratic schools* (pp. 83–100). Alexandria, VA: Association for Supervision and Curriculum Development.

Brown, C. G. (2005). *Postmodernism for historians.* Harlow, UK: Pearson Longman.

Centers for Disease Control and Prevention. (2011). Injury center: Violence prevention. national suicide statistics at a glance. Retrieved from http://www.cdc.gov/violence prevention/ suicide/ statistics.

Changing Times. (1982, June). When a teenager gets really depressed. *36,* 27–28.

Chaplain, S. (2010). *American schools: The art of creating a democratic learning community.* Lanham, MD: Rowman & Littlefield.

Child, L. M. (1839). "Lydia Marie Child: Selected letters." In J. A. Marone (Ed.), *Hellfire nation: The politics of sin in American history* (pp. 169–70). New Haven, CT: Yale University Press.

Cohen, A. P. (1989). *The symbolic construction of community.* New York, NY: Routledge.

Currie, M. (1998). *Postmodern narrative theory.* New York, NY: Palgrave.

Curry, A. (2004, April). Flower Child. *Smithsonian Magazine.* https://www.smithsonianmag.com/history/flower-child-102514360/.

Dewey, John. (1964). *Selected writings.* Reginald D. & Ed. Armchambault (Eds.). New York, NY: Modern Library Books/Random House.

Dewey, John. (2005). *Democracy and education.* New York, NY: Barnes & Noble.

Dickens, C. (2006). *Oliver Twist.* New York, NY: Barnes & Noble.

Dickinson, E. (1993). *The collected poems of Emily Dickinson.* New York, NY: Barnes & Noble.

Dinkmeyer, D., & Dreikurs, R. (1963). *Encouraging children to learn: The encouragement process.* Englewood Cliffs, NJ: Prentice-Hall.

Dinkmeyer, D., & McKay, G. D. (1973). *Raising a responsible child.* New York, NY: Simon & Schuster.

Dinkmeyer, D., McKay, G., & Dinkmeyer, D., Jr. (1980). *Systematic training for effective teaching.* Circle Pines, MN: American Guidance Service.

Dreikurs, R., & Cassel P. (1972). *Discipline without tears.* New York, NY: Penguin.

Dreikurs, R. (1972). *Dreikurs Sayings: Texts from the works of Rudolph Dreikurs.* Compiled by Theo Shoenaker and Eva Dreikurs Ferguson. Cambridge: Icassi Publishing, 168.

Dreikurs, R., Grunwald, B. B., & Pepper, F. (1982). *Maintaining sanity in the classroom.* New York, NY: Harper & Row.

Dreikurs, R. & Stoltz, V. (1964). *Children: The Challenge.* New York: E. P. Dutton.

Dreikurs, R. (1950). *Fundamentals of Adlerian Psychology.* Out of print.

Egan, S. J., &Wade, T. D. (2010). Perfectionism as a trans diagnostic process: A clinical review. *Clinical Psychology Review, 31,* 203–12.

Emerson, R. W. (2010). *Self-reliance: The over-soul and other essays.* Claremont, CA: Coyote Canyon Press.

Esteva, G., & Prakash, M. S. (1998). *Grassroots postmodernism: Remaking the soils of cultures.* London, UK: Zed Books.

Fass, P. S. (2016). *The end of American childhood.* Princeton, NJ: Princeton University Press.

Fairholm, G. (1998). *Perspectives on leadership: From the science of management to its spiritual heart.* Westport, CT: Quorum Books.

Fetner, T., & Elafros, A. (2015). The GSA difference: LGBTQ and ally experiences in high schools with and without gay-straight alliances, *Social Science, 4*(3). Retrieved from http://www.mdpi.com/2076–0760/4/3/563.

Fisher, M. (1897). "A Student's 'Goodbye' Suicide Shocks D.C. Junior High School." March 26. *Washington Post.*

Foucault, M. (1989). *Foucault live (interviews, 1961–1984).* Sylvester Lotringer (Ed.). New York, NY: Semiotexte.

Frost, S. E. (1962). *Basic teaching of the great philosophers.* New York, NY: Anchor Books.

Furman, G. (2002). *School as community: From promise to practice.* Albany, NY: State University of New York Press.

Furtak, R. A. (2019). Henry David Thoreau. In *The Stanford Encyclopedia of Philosophy*, ed. E. N. Zalta. https://plato.stanford.edu/archives/fall2019/entries/thoreau.

Garrison, W. L. (1938). *Letters of William Lloyd Garrison.* Vol. 1: *A house dividing against itself, 1836–1840.* L. Ruchames (Ed.). Cambridge, MA: Belknap Press.

Glasser W. (1986). *Control Theory in the classroom.* New York: Harper & Row. 56.

Gottman, J. (1997). *Raising an emotionally intelligent child.* New York, NY: Fireside.

Griffith, J., & Powers, R. (2007). *The lexicon of Adlerian Psychology: 106 terms associated with the individual psychology of Alfred Adler* (2nd ed.). Port Townsend ,WA: Adlerian Psychology Associates, Ltd.

Hakim, J. (1993). *From colonies to country: 1735–1791.* New York, NY: Oxford University Press.

Hicks, S. R. C. (2011). *Explaining postmodernism: Skepticism and socialism from Rousseau to Foucault.* Roscoe, IL: Ockham's Razor.

Hindman, Hugh D. (2002) *Child labor: An American history.* New York, NY: M. E. Sharpe.

Hitchcock, R. A. (1987). Understanding physical abuse as a life-style. *Journal of Individual Psychology*, *43*, 50–55.

Hume, D. (1888). *A treatise of human nature.* London, UK: Clarendon Press.

Jacob, M. C. (2001). *The Enlightenment: A brief history with documents.* Boston, MA: Bedford/St. Martin's.

James, S. D. (2014, January 21). Oregon boy's bucket list: feed the homeless. ABC News. Retrieved from https://abcnews.go.com/Health/dying-oregon-boys-bucket-list-feed-homeless/story?id=21601597.

Joiner, T. E. (2005). *Why people die by suicide.* Cambridge, MA: Harvard University Press.

Kant, I. (1954). What is the enlightenment? (Gay, P., Trans.). In *Introduction to contemporary civilization in the west*: a source book. Vol. 1. New York, NY: Columbia University Press.

KCRA News. (2005, April 20). Students campaign to stop BB gun sales at ice cream trucks. Retrieved from https://www.kcra.com/article/students-campaign-to-stop-bb-gun-sales-at-ice-cream-trucks/6363926.

Kennedy A. (2015). *The US Supreme Court decision on marriage equality.* New York, NY: Melville House.

Kozol, J. (1991). *Savage inequalities: Children in America's schools.* New York, NY: Crown Press.

Levine, E. (1993). *Freedom's children.* New York, NY: Penguin.

Lombardi, D. N., Florentino, M. C., and Lombardi, A. J. (1998). Perfectionism and Abmormal Behavior. *Individual Psychology*, *54*(1), 61.

Lundkin, R. (1989). *Alfred Adler's basic concepts and implications.* Levitown, Taylor & Francis Group, 39–40.

Magee, B. (1998). *The story of philosophy.* London, UK: Dorling Kindersley.

Manion, J. (2002). *Essentials of philosophy.* New York, NY: Fall River Press.

Maxwell, W. (2018, March 22). Law enforcement wasn't the first to fail in the Parkland school shooting. LifeSiteNews. Retrieved from https://www.lifesitenews.com/opinion/law-enforcement-wasnt-the-first-to-fail-in-the-parkland-school-shooting.

McCullough, D. (2001). *John Adams.* New York: Simon & Schuster, 65.

McNamara, P. (2011, September 7). Johnny Clem: The drummer boy of Chickamauga. Patheos. Retrieved from https://www.patheos.com/blogs/mcnamarasblog/2011/09/johnny-clem-"the-drummer-boy-of-chickamauga".html.

Marone, James A., (2003). *Hellfire Nation.* New Haven: Yale University Press, 444.

Matthews, C. J. (2017). *Bobby Kennedy: A raging spirit.* New York, NY: Simon & Schuster.

McCullough, D. (2001). *John Adams.* New York, NY: Simon & Schuster.

McCullough, D. (2005). *1776.* New York, NY: Simon & Schuster.

Meier, D. (1995). *The power of their ideas: Lessons for America from a small school in Harlem.* Boston, MA: Beacon Press.

Mosak, H., & Maniacci, M. (1999). *A primer of Adlerian psychology: The analytic-behavioral-cognitive psychology of Alfred Adler.* New York, NY: Brunner Rutledge.

Mullenbach, C. (2014). *Industrial Revolution for Kids*. Chicago: Chicago Review Press.

Mullenbach, C. (2015). *The Great Depression for Kids*Chicago: Chicago Review Press.

NBC News. (2014, September 14). Teen invents sensor to help Alzheimer's patients. Retrieved from https://www.nbcnews.com/feature/making-a-difference/teen-invents-sensor-help-alzheimers-patients-n203231.

Nelsen, J., Lott, L., & Glenn, H. S. (1997). *Positive discipline in the classroom*. Rocklin, CA: Prima.

Newman, K. S., Fox, C., Harding. D., Mehta, J., & Roth, W. (2005). *Rampage: The social roots of school shootings*. New York, NY: Perseus Books.

O'Toole, M. E. (1999). *The school shooter: A threat assessment perspective*. Retrieved from https://www.fbi.gov/file-repository/stats-services-publications-school-shooter-school-shooter/view.

Rose, J., and Booker, B. (2018, March 1). Parkland shooting suspect: A story of red flags, ignored. *All things considered* [Radio broadcast]. Washington, DC: National Public Radio. Retrieved from https://www.npr.org/2018/02/28/589502906/a-clearer-picture-of-parkland-shooting-suspect-comes-into-focus.

Powell, J. (1998). *Postmodernism for beginners*. New York, NY: Writers and Readers.

Quarles, B. (1969) *Black abolitionists*. New York, NY: Oxford University Press.

Remarque, E. M. (1929/1982). *All quiet on the western front*. New York, NY: Random House.

Richmond, E. (2015, December 29). When restorative justice in schools works. *Atlantic*. Retrieved from https://www.theatlantic.com/education/archive/2015/12/when-restorative-justice-works/422088/.

Roderick, M., M. Arney, M. Axelman, et al. (1997, July). *Habits hard to break: A new look at truancy in Chicago's public schools*. University of Chicago, School of Social Service Administration. Retrieved from https://consortium.uchicago.edu/sites/default/files/2018-10/p0a09.pdf.

Rodriguez, M., & Ashton, J. (2010, January 28). Four days after learning to dial 9-1-1 in an emergency, 3-year-old Jaden Bolli saved his grandmother's life. CBS News. Retrieved from https://www.youtube.com/watch?v=KF43Y3kBzas.

Rorty, R. (1998). *Achieving our country: Leftist thought in twentieth-century America*. Cambridge, MA: Harvard University Press.

Rose, J. and Booker, B. (2018). Parkland shooting suspect: A story of red flags, ignored. March 1. NPR. Retrieved from https://www.npr.org/2018/02/28/589502906/a-clearer-picture-of-parkland-shooting-suspect-comes-into-focus.

Rousseau, J. J. (2011). *Basic political writings*. Indianapolis, IN: Hackett.

Sandel, M. (2012). *What money can't buy ?* New York, NY: Farrar, Straus and Giroux.

Segarra, L. M. (2018, March 24). Here are the most powerful speeches from March For Our Lives in Washington. *Time*. https://time.com/5214452/march-for-our-lives-best-speeches/.

Sergiovanni, T. J. (1992). *Moral leadership: Getting to the heart of school improvement*. San Francisco, CA: Jossey-Bass.

Sergiovanni, T. J. (1994). *Building community in schools*. San Francisco, CA: Jossey-Bass.

Sinclair, U. (1906). *The Jungle*. New York, NY: Bantam Dell.

Slattery, P. (1995). *Curriculum development in the postmodern era*. New York, NY: Garland.

Spears, L. C. (Ed.). (1998). *Insights on leadership*. New York, NY: Wiley.

Steinbeck, J. (1939). *The grapes of wrath*. New York, NY: Viking.

Thoreau, H. D. (1995). *Walden; or, life in the woods*. Mineola, NY: Dover Publications.

Turck, M. (2000). *The civil rights movement for kids*. Chicago, IL: Chicago Review Press.

Trattner, W. I. (1970). *Crusade for children: A history of the national child labor committee and child labor reform in America*. Chicago, IL: Quadrangle.

Updike, J. (1960). *Rabbit, run*. New York, NY: Knopf.

Walters, R. G. (1976). *Anti-slavery Appeal*. New York, NY: Norton.

Walton, F. (1988). "Teenage suicide:An approach to prevention." *Individual Psychology: The Journal of Adlerian Theory, Research & Practice*. Austin: University of Texas Press.

Watkins, T. H. (1993). *The great depression: America in the 1930's*. Boston, MA: Little, Brown.

Whitman, W. (2005). *Song of myself: A source book and critical edition*. E. Greenspan (Ed.). New York, NY: Routledge.

Wiesel, E. (1958/2006). *Night*. New York, NY: Hill and Wang.

Wiseman, C. V., Gray, J. J., Mosimann, J. E., & Ahrens, A. H. (1992). Cultural expectations of thinness in women: An update. *International Journal of Eating Disorders, 111*, 85–89.

WND. (2007, March 3). School kids' march in "gay" parade protested. Retrieved from https://www.wnd.com/2007/03/40455/.

Wolfgang, C. H., & Glickman, C. D. (1986). *Solving discipline problems: Strategies for classroom teachers*. Newton, MA: Allyn & Bacon.

Wordsworth, W. (1994). *The collected poems of William Wordsworth*. Hertfordshire, UK: Wordsworth Editions.

Vitousek, K. B., & Hollon, S. D. (1990). The investigation of schematic content and processing in eating disorders. *Cognitive Therapy and Research, 14*, 191–214.

Young, L. (1965) *Life among the giants: A child's-eye view of the grown-up world*. New York, NY: McGraw Hill.

Index